ASK LIKE YOU MEAN IT

LESSONS IN COMMUNICATION FROM AN UNEXPECTED SOURCE, MY HORSE!

MARIA ALESSANDRI

Copyright © 2026 Maria Alessandri

Published by Back Fields Farm, LLC

All rights reserved. No part of this publication may be reproduced, distributed, or transmitted in any form or by any means, electronic or mechanical, including photocopying, recording, or any information storage and retrieval system, without the prior written permission of the publisher. Requests to the publisher for permission should be addressed to maria@horseandpeopleproject.com.

ISBN 979-8-9931222-0-5 (Paperback)
ISBN 979-8-9931222-1-2 (EBook)

Book Design & Layout: Toni Serofin, Sanserofin Studio

*What shall I return to the Lord
for all his goodness to me?*
~Psalm 116:12 ~

*There is something about the outside of a horse
that is good for the inside of a man.*
~ Winston S. Churchill ~

*The single biggest problem in communication
is the illusion that it has taken place.*
~ Attributed to George Bernard Shaw ~

DISCLAIMER 1

For the privacy of the individuals involved, names, genders and/or identifying characteristics have been changed. Names of horses have not been changed.

DISCLAIMER 2

This book is filled with leadership and parenting advice, but my colleagues and children could tell you about the times I've fallen short. As a curious seeker and self-help enthusiast, I'm always learning about human interactions and striving to grow along the way.

About this Book

Over the past five years, I've hosted hundreds of sessions at my farm, *Back Fields Farm LLC*, in a small town in Maryland. Individuals have come to learn, not about horses, but about themselves, through the honest, nonverbal feedback of my equine partners. This book is rooted in the lessons I've learned and stories I've collected over the past few years through my coaching work at the *Horse and People Project*, an initiative I established at my farm.

In 2024, I began accepting public speaking engagements to share these lessons learned, knowing that not everyone can make it out to the farm, but that everyone can benefit from the wisdom of horses. The response has been overwhelmingly positive, and in the process, I found I thoroughly enjoy being a storyteller and public speaker.

That encouragement led me to write this book.

It's a collection of real-life stories; from parents who learned how to connect more meaningfully with their kids, to leaders who suddenly saw how their energy and body language were impacting their teams. Woven throughout are my own stories as well, my experiences as a mother of five, a former corporate professional, and a lifelong student of both human and animal behavior.

As a self-help enthusiast with a fascination for animals in general, and horses specifically, I've long been inspired by the likes of Brené Brown and Temple Grandin, researchers and storytellers who blend science, emotion, and actionable insight. This book aims to do the same. It's a lofty goal, I know!

The lessons shared here are simple, relatable, and often deeply moving. From "My Daughter's Tattoo" to "The Big Boss," each story offers a message about communication, connection, and what it means to truly lead. Whether you're parenting a teenager or managing a team, the same themes apply: those of clarity, consistency, authenticity, and compassion.

Communication is the key to healthy relationships. Learning from a horse is just plain fun. Their size adds to the wonder; when a horse listens to you, really listens and responds, you feel it, deep down inside. The experience has been described by many as awe-inspiring, profound, and life changing. It's been noted for its simplicity, yet the impact it leaves is undeniable, resonating deeply with those who have participated in a session or attended a presentation.

Ultimately, this book is for anyone who wants to build stronger, more resilient relationships, at home, at work, and everywhere in between. My goal is for these stories to inspire readers to listen more closely, lead more clearly, and live more intentionally. This book isn't meant to be a heavy or academic read; it's a light, engaging, and practical guide filled with relatable stories and down-to-earth insights. I've included reflection prompts at the end of the chapters, encouraging the reader to consider for themselves how they show up in relationships. My hope is that readers will not only enjoy it, but also recognize themselves within its pages.

The title, *Ask Like You Mean It*, comes from something I found myself saying often during sessions, and it became a mantra of sorts. When individuals and groups come out to the farm, I guide them through four core exercises in a round pen with a loose horse. Each exercise mirrors real-life communication patterns: for example, the way a person asks a horse to move can reveal their ability to set clear intentions and follow through. All the work is done on the ground; there is no horseback riding involved. At first, many participants are hesitant; they approach too softly and without intention. When they ask the horse for movement, I remind them to "Ask Like You Mean It."

Throughout the book are insights into horse psychology, helping readers understand not just what we do in the round pen, but why it works. At the most basic level, horses are prey animals and humans are predators—two species that shouldn't naturally get along. And yet, horses choose to engage with us and offer their wisdom. They reach places in us that we often are unaware of, offering honest, nonjudgmental feedback in gentle (usually) and profound ways.

Table of Contents

About this Book	v
Preface: Boy Scouts Visit the Farm	xi
SECTION I: Horse and People Project at Back Fields Farm	**1**
Getting There	3
Horse Psychology	5
Lost Babies	7
Runaway Horse	8
Runaway Son	10
Thoughts on Anger/Parenting Fail	12
Pilot or Passenger?	14
Approach and Retreat	16
SECTION II: My Favorite Classroom	**19**
The Round Pen	21
The Science	23
There's No Crying in Horse Training	26
Mirror, Mirror on the Wall	27
Too Intense	29
It's Hard to Change!	32
Content or Delivery?	34
Finding Neutral	36
Can't Stop Yawning	39
SECTION III: Round Pen Sessions	**43**
Exercise 1: The Back-Up	45
Releasing Pressure	47
Where Is Your Energy Going?	48
You Can't Make Me	50
Split Energy	51

Exercise 2: The Send	53
Lead from Behind	55
Is Anybody Listening?	57
My Daughter's Tattoo	60
The Big Boss	62
Lick and Chew (Couples Therapy!)	66
Too Noisy	68
Exercise 3: The Leg	71
Ask Like You Mean It	72
Can I Say No?	74
Was That a Question?	77
Tug of War	78
Ask, Don't Bribe	81
Exercise 4: The Magnet	85
That's Not How Humans Walk	87
Block, Don't Punch	89
Why Trick Him?	93
Don't Worry, He's Following	94
SECTION IV: Stories from Clients	99
SECTION V: Looking Ahead	113
Continuing the Journey	115
Resources	119
Acknowledgements	123
About the Author	125

PREFACE

Boy Scouts Visit the Farm

Years ago, while sitting in the dentist's chair, I found myself animatedly describing my latest passion: natural horsemanship. I'd been playing the role of "horse whisperer" for a while, and my excitement was hard to contain. The dental practice, a small office of five women, was familiar and friendly from my regular visits for myself and my five kids and had become a place where casual conversations often turned personal. We talked about everyday life, our families, our homes, motherhood, schools, camps, food, and hobbies.

As I shared stories of the breakthroughs I was having with my beloved horse, Ace, my dentist listened with genuine interest. Midway through my exam, she paused and mentioned that her husband led a Boy Scout Troop. With a spark of inspiration, she asked if I'd be willing to host them for a visit to the farm and demonstrate some of the techniques I'd been raving about.

Excited to show off Ace and my new skills, I readily agreed. The idea of connecting people, especially children, with the beauty of horses and the subtle magic of gentle communication was too good to pass up.

Plans were made and a date was set. A lively group arrived made up of about a dozen young boys, ages ten to twelve, accompanied by five or six parents and the troop leader, my dentist's husband. The boys excitedly piled out of the cars; I could tell they were happy to be out at a farm. The parents, not fully knowing what they were in for, were curious and open.

To start, I led them on a tour of the barn, introducing them to some of the equine residents. The boys as well as the parents enjoyed getting to pet the horses while I told them a little about some of the horses under my care. The boys were particularly interested in the grain bin and what the horses liked to eat. I let them each hold a handful of the sweet feed and instructed them, with their hands held open and fingers flat, how to offer a little snack to the horses that had come into their stalls. The boys were also interested in the tack room, where all the saddles, bridles and grooming equipment are kept. It's one of my favorite rooms, smelling of leather and Mane 'n Tail shampoo.

After the barn tour, I guided them toward the round pen where Ace was patiently waiting, taking the opportunity to graze on the fresh springtime grass. I had taken extra care in our grooming routine in anticipation of the afternoon's visitors. I felt excited and proud to introduce Ace, the horse who had become my greatest teacher.

As I began the demonstration, I spoke not just of technique but of relationship, the subtle language of partnership I had cultivated with Ace. I described how I had learned to be present for him, creating a safe and steady space he could rely on. I shared how I showed up every day for him, through good weather and bad, being a consistent and steady source of support in his life. I related the way I had learned to guide Ace through moments of uncertainty or fear (and he had a lot of them!) with calm reassurance.

I explained the responsibilities that came with owning a horse: feeding, grooming, and cleaning stalls, the basic duties of animal husbandry. In return, Ace gave me more than I could have expected or imagined. He taught me to let go of stress and to release tension I didn't even know I was carrying. He taught me to let go of frustration and anger and to not hold grudges. He showed me that authenticity wasn't a weakness, but a strength. He taught me to be more honest and vulnerable, that I didn't have to pretend to know more than I did, or be stronger than I was. I learned to lead without force, with clarity, steadiness, and grace, a true partnership.

The response from the scouts was about what I expected: they wanted to know Ace's favorite treats, which stall was his, who his field mates were, and what a typical day was like for him. Their questions were sweet and innocent, their attention span short. They were ready to move onto the next adventure, soon running around the farm.

But the parents—the parents were listening differently. I noticed how they nodded with quiet recognition as I shared stories of parenting fails and frustrations. When I described how working with Ace had made me a more patient and present mother, a better leader, and a better co-worker, I caught glimpses of reflection on their faces. They weren't just hearing a story about a horse; they were hearing something about themselves.

What I thought would be a learning experience for the boys turned out to be something far deeper for the parents. It was one of the first moments I realized the power of the lessons that Ace and my other horses had taught me. Their wisdom wasn't just for equestrians, it was for anyone willing to listen. That day planted the seed for what would become the *Horse and People Project*. I realized that even people who never touched a horse could still learn from them, whether by working alongside them or simply by hearing their stories.

SECTION I

Horse and People Project at Back Fields Farm

How we show up matters, whether with horses, children, friends, family, or colleagues. This section is an introduction to how horses respond to us and how they can help us learn about ourselves. We learn the importance of slowing down, noticing our own energy, and becoming conscious of our patterns and presence.

Getting There

When clients first visit Back Fields Farm, they're immediately struck by the beauty of the setting. Tucked away on the back 20 acres of a sprawling 500-acre farm, reaching the barn is part of the adventure. For many, it's their first time driving on farm roads, expecting GPS to lead them right to the door, except my barn doesn't have its own address. I simply call it the back 20.

As they wind their way down the two-mile dirt lane, the sheer size of the farm starts to sink in. They pass the pond on the left, where in the summer, lucky visitors might spot swans giving their babies flying lessons. Last year, there were five cygnets. From there, they take a right at the first tobacco barn, follow the road past the weathered cinder block tractor building, and weave between two more tobacco barns. Finally, they drive alongside fields of corn (or soybeans, depending on the year) for another mile until they dead-end at Back Fields Farm, the heart of the Horse and People Project.

Clients have told me that by the time they make their way down the lane and arrive at my barn, they already feel different; something has shifted. The quiet, the openness, and the rhythm of the landscape seem to promote settled, calm feelings. Nearly everyone comments on how peaceful it feels, making it an ideal setting for the work we are about to do.

To ease into the experience, I usually start with a walk through the ten-stall pole barn, introducing them to some of the four-legged residents. The stalls, with their open fronts and back doors leading to the pastures, give the horses the freedom to come and go as they please. If they're feeling social, they wander over to say hello, stretching their necks to greet curious hands, and of course hoping to receive treats.

Most of the horses are rescues, saved and adopted by caring owners. Spending a few moments touching the horses, feeling the warmth of their coats, and hearing their backstories (if we know their history), helps the clients start to see the animals as individuals, with quirks and personalities as distinct as any human's. Having this initial interaction with the horses helps the visitors and clients feel comfortable and start thinking of the horses as friends and partners, not just animals to ride. There's the introvert who prefers to hang back, the clown who's always nudging for attention, and, of course, the spoiled one who demands affection. Most clients are surprised by how personable the horses are, having never had the chance to know one up close, especially in a setting where they can be themselves.

Even though the horses live in captivity, I strive to keep their environment as natural as possible. They are free to stay in their herds, not locked into stalls or separated. Their diet consists mostly of grass and hay, supplemented with grain only to replace the nutrients they can't forage for themselves. I let their winter coats grow thick rather than blanketing them, even if it means dealing with the inevitable springtime shedding spree. And I don't put shoes on them; it's not necessary, since they live on soft ground.

Each pasture holds a small group of four to six horses, and they establish their own hierarchy. At feeding time, I honor their natural order, starting with the dominant horse and working my way down the pecking order. But when I step into the field, the dynamic changes; I become the leader. This is essential for safety. Too often, well-meaning horse owners walk into a pasture with treats, unaware of the potential danger. In a field full of horses, food can quickly lead to squabbles, and getting caught in the middle is never safe.

Horse Psychology

Humans are predators; horses are prey. By nature, we shouldn't be friends. Yet, we are incredibly fortunate that horses are willing to trust us, to work alongside us, and sometimes, even more astonishingly, to form deep bonds with us.

As predators, humans tend to be aggressive, often without realizing it. So many of our everyday movements and behaviors are inherently predatory. Actions we barely think about, but which horses feel instantly. Our eyes, positioned front and center on our faces, give us a direct and penetrating gaze. To another human, eye contact may signal confidence or connection. But to a horse, that same stare can feel threatening, like a lion locking onto its next meal.

People are often intimidated by horses because of their size, their towering frames, powerful muscles, and quick, unpredictable movements. But what many don't realize is that horses have no predatory instincts. Their first response to fear is not to fight; it's to run. Speed and distance are their greatest defenses. Fighting is their last resort, and even then, it's rarely the whole herd. Usually, only one member will stand its ground, giving the others a chance to flee.

Humans on the other hand, have the ability to assess danger and decide whether to fight or run, a dual instinct of fight-or-flight. We can pause, evaluate, and choose our response. Horses don't have that luxury. Their only instinct is flight. When they hear an unfamiliar rustle or catch a glimpse of a fleeting shadow, they don't stop to weigh the odds, they run. And with four legs built for speed, they can cover a lot of ground in a very short time.

A horse's eyes, positioned on the sides of its head, provide a wide field of vision. Even as they graze with their heads down, they remain vigilant, scanning for potential threats. This near-constant state of awareness is the key to their survival; it allows them to detect movement and danger from nearly every angle without ever having to lift their heads.

All these traits make working with horses incredibly exciting, and deeply rewarding. The interactions are 100% honest, with no room for pretense. Horses don't care about your title, your appearance, or your words. They respond only to your energy, intention, and authenticity. Horses have no ulterior motives. I often say, "horses don't play chess." What I mean by that is simply that horses live in the moment, they do not have a set of moves and counter-moves ready to block, deflect, or beat us.

This raw honesty creates a powerful mirror, reflecting our own ways of being and interacting with others. When we work with horses, we're forced to become more self-aware. If we're anxious or scattered, they'll know it. If we're calm and centered, they'll trust us. Their feedback is instant and unfiltered, offering us a rare opportunity for genuine self-reflection and growth.

Lost Babies

A few years ago, two foals (baby horses) were found loose in my neighborhood. When my neighbors were unable to catch or even approach the frightened babies, they called me, knowing I had horses and might be able to help. Without hesitation, I grabbed some halters and ropes, hopped in my truck, and drove through the neighborhood until I spotted a small crowd gathered in a neighbor's front yard. The foals were grazing, but the tension in the air was unmistakable. Everyone was worried the youngsters would wander toward the main road, where they could easily be hit by a passing car.

As I approached, I could see right away that the foals were scared and ready to bolt. Their wide eyes and twitching ears revealed how uncomfortable they were around people; these babies clearly hadn't been handled much, if at all. I tried a direct approach at first, moving toward them with slow, deliberate steps, but it was too much. They spooked immediately and dashed into the next yard. The only thing keeping them from disappearing entirely was the lure of the lush green grass.

Realizing I needed a different strategy, I softened my body language and began following them in a roundabout, meandering pattern. I even walked backward at times, careful to reduce the straight-line, predatory energy that made them feel threatened. Thankfully, this approach worked! The foals, sensing less pressure, allowed me to inch closer, until I was near enough to gently toss the ropes around their necks. Instead of rushing them, I stood still and let them continue grazing. I wanted them to feel safe and not trapped before attempting to lead them anywhere.

While I stayed with the foals, one of my neighbors managed to contact their owner, who quickly made her way over. When she arrived, I carefully guided the babies toward her, bringing them to the entrance of the woods, a natural shortcut that would take them back to their barn, about a mile away.

What happened next was disappointing. The owner, clearly frazzled by the ordeal, grabbed the ropes and immediately started walking into the woods with a forceful, aggressive energy. Her sharp movements and mounting frustration startled the foals, who panicked and tore free, bolting and disappearing into the trees.

I watched helplessly as she stood there, flustered and empty-handed. Her impatience had torn apart the fragile trust I'd worked to build. At that point, I hoped the foals' instincts would guide them home safely, but I knew the situation could have ended more positively.

That day, I learned a powerful lesson: when someone is set on using an ineffective approach, it's incredibly hard to change their mind. No matter how much care or progress you've made, if frustration takes over, it can undo any progress in an instant.

Runaway Horse

Years ago, before I opened my own barn, I boarded my two horses, Ace and Cisco, at a farm near my house. With five kids to raise and part-time work keeping me busy, my visits to the barn were precious. I would steal away whenever I had a spare moment, eager for the peace and connection I felt being at the farm and around my horses.

At that farm, there was a young woman who owned a mare (adult female horse). I noticed something odd: the mare always wore a halter and lead rope around her head, even when she was loose in the pasture. Most horses graze freely without any gear, so I was curious. When I asked the owner why she kept the halter on, she explained that her mare often ran away from her. The halter was her quick fix, a way to grab the mare when she needed to bring her in. She would try to entice her mare with treats, and then when she was within a foot of her, the young woman would quickly grab the rope and force her mare to follow.

To me, this didn't feel right. It was the opposite of the relationship I wanted with my horses. I didn't want to have to catch them against their will, I wanted them to want to be caught. I wanted my horses to see me and come running, like my dog excitedly greeting me at the door. It would be awful if my dog ran away from me every time I came home! And yet this is unfortunately all too common in the horse world. I decided to do things differently, and it paid off.

One day, as I was driving onto the farm, I spotted my two horses galloping toward the gate to greet me. They were so excited; I couldn't get to the gate fast enough for them! The young woman happened to be there and saw the whole thing. She was stunned. She asked if it was a fluke or if they always did that. I smiled and told her it was no accident; they always came to meet me. I never had to chase them down or trick them into being with me.

She was curious; she wanted to know how I made that happen. I explained that I had spent an entire month simply showing up for my horses. Not just to ride them or make demands of them, but to be with them. I had focused on building a relationship rooted in trust and positive experiences.

Some days, I rode. Other days, I took them out for grazing adventures, gave them baths, or spoiled them with their favorite treats. Of course, there were less pleasant days too, when the vet, dentist, or farrier came. But I made sure to balance those necessary, sometimes uncomfortable experiences with enjoyable ones. By keeping things varied and making sure they associated me with comfort, safety, and fun, not just work or stress, I earned their trust.

As a result, they were always happy to see me. They wanted to be with me. That is the kind of relationship worth my time and effort.

Unfortunately, the young woman's response was, "That's too much work." Her words stuck with me. I was disappointed, but I understood there was nothing I could do about it. Building a genuine relationship, with a horse (or a human), is work. It takes time, patience, and consistency. To me, it is always worth it.

Runaway Son

A few years later, I was sitting at my kitchen counter, sipping my morning coffee, when out of the corner of my eye I saw one of my teenage sons walking toward the kitchen. As soon as he noticed me, he hesitated. He quickly backed up, hoping I hadn't spotted him, trying to sneak away.

That's when it hit me.

I was doing to my son exactly what that young woman had done to her mare. Without realizing it, I had made our relationship so one-sided, so transactional, that he didn't want to be around me. During his teenage years, I often worried about him falling behind, missing assignments, leaving laundry undone, ignoring college applications, and so on. Because he wasn't one to share much, I would pepper him with questions every time I saw him. "Did you get your homework done? Have you cleaned your room? Did you send in your essay?" To him, I had become the person who only showed up when I needed something or wanted to check on his progress. It was no wonder he was backing away.

But my experience with my horses gave me the insight I needed. I could do something to repair and improve my relationship with my son, just as I had done with my horses. I needed to reverse the dynamic. With my horses, I learned that showing up just to ride or demand something from them created resistance. But showing up consistently, offering comfort, safety, and companionship, built trust and strengthened our bond. I asked myself: How could I show up for my son?

Of course, carrots and grazing time wouldn't work in this case. But I knew the same principles could apply. I made a conscious decision: for the next ten interactions with him (at the very least), I would be completely nonjudgmental and free of expectations. No questions that felt like prying. No disguised "to-do list" prompts.

Instead, I asked about things that didn't come with pressure, things like the latest books, movies, or music that he was interested in. When we were in the car, I didn't grill him for information. Sometimes, I'd simply say, "Do you mind if I finish this audio book I've been listening to?" With horses, I learned that walking away or turning your back could release pressure and bring comfort. I wondered if the same could work with my son. So, I tried it. I intentionally became the one to leave a conversation or room first, making space instead of clinging, thereby releasing the pressure.

I was relieved to see that it helped. Bit by bit, the tension eased. Treating my son as an interesting person with his own thoughts and ideas, rather than a project I needed to manage, was just the beginning.

All relationships, especially the ones we have with our children, need to evolve. We start by changing their diapers, making every decision for them, and being in control of their entire world. But as they grow, we have to let them take the reins, little by little. We have to create space for them to make their own choices, even when it's hard to let go.

At my kitchen counter that morning I realized I needed to make more space for my son, to stop managing him and start being present with him. It wasn't easy, and it's still something I work on to this day. Just like with my horses, building trust meant showing up, not only when I wanted something or when there was work to be done, but simply to be present. To share space. To listen. And to let go.

Thoughts on Anger/Parenting Fail

When one of my daughters was about seven or eight, she was riding her bicycle around the neighborhood and fell. Her knee was badly scraped and bleeding, and she needed stitches. I was out running errands when the babysitter called. I rushed home, anxious and afraid of what I would find.

But when I walked through the door and saw my daughter, her face pale with pain, blood running down her leg, the first thing I did was yell at her.

"I told you to be careful on that hill!"

My fear, without any pause for reflection, had morphed into anger. My poor daughter, who had been keeping it together so bravely until that point, burst into tears. She didn't need scolding; she needed her mom to wrap her in a hug and tell her everything would be okay. Instead, my misplaced anger made things worse.

That moment stayed with me. It was one of the first times I realized how easily fear can turn into anger. In fact, many emotions, frustration, uncertainty, and even hunger, can mask themselves as anger. But if we focus only on the anger, we miss the mark. We miss the chance to address what's really going on underneath.

I've seen this same pattern with my horses. If one of them spooks on the trail and starts to act up, my natural reaction is to grab the reins tightly and tense up with fear. If I let that fear turn into frustration or anger, it doesn't help my horse relax. It's often a natural reaction to try to control with aggression, but this only makes things worse. My tension confirms to my horse that there is indeed something to fear. The result is a vicious cycle of escalating fear—exactly the opposite of what either of us needs.

With horses, I've learned the power of detaching from reactive emotions. When I stay calm and steady, my horse feels it. My composure gives him a reason to feel safe. My steady presence, my calm confidence, becomes the anchor we both need.

This is a lesson I still need to practice. My natural tendency is to let fear and frustration turn into anger. It takes constant practice (and plenty of self-forgiveness) to remind myself that it's okay. I'm still learning. Still growing.

In life, I try to apply the same lesson. I work on detaching from other people's emotional rollercoasters. That doesn't mean I don't empathize or care deeply; it just means I don't have to be swept away by their storm. By holding steady, I can be a safe space, which makes me more helpful and more present.

Pilot or Passenger?

A few years ago, I inherited a horse at my barn named Ben. One of my boarders had adopted him and loved him very much but found herself overwhelmed with life and felt she couldn't give him the time and attention he deserved. She asked if I would adopt him, and I happily agreed. I had recently lost my longtime riding horse, Lucas, to old age, as he had lived well into his thirties. While I don't include riding in my Horse and People program, I still personally enjoy the experience and the deeper connection it offers.

Ben is a big horse, part Belgian draft, weighing about 1200 pounds (think plow horse). Despite his size, he's surprisingly sensitive and quite insecure. Ben used to be great on the trails, sure-footed, calm, and reliable. But a while ago, something changed. He began acting up. He spooked easily, became agitated, and wanted to bolt back to the barn. It came on suddenly, and given his size and strength, it was intimidating.

Concerned, his then-owner had him tested for Lyme disease. Sure enough, the results were positive. Lyme can cause a range of symptoms in horses: behavioral shifts, joint soreness, increased sensitivity, even changes in vision. He underwent a full month of treatment, and while that helped, it didn't restore him to his pre-diagnosis self. When he became mine, I knew I would need to put in extra time to help him regain his confidence through supplements, groundwork, round pen exercises, and carefully structured riding sessions.

According to Temple Grandin, world-renowned animal behaviorist, "(a) horse is a sensory-based visual thinker, and fear is its main emotion" (from her book, Animals Make Us Human). As previously discussed, horses, as prey animals, don't usually fight when threatened; they run. That's their nature. So, when a horse like Ben feels scared or unsure, his instinct is to escape. If I ignore his fear, hoping he'll just "get over it," I risk making things worse. But if I acknowledge his fear and offer calm leadership, I give him the opportunity to find balance again.

That's where the concept of being the pilot or the passenger comes in.

I've learned that Ben becomes unsettled when I take a passive role. He believes he wants independence but becomes anxious when left entirely to his own decisions. If I hesitate or lack clarity, whether on the ground or in the saddle, he feels unsure. He needs me to be decisive. He feels safest when I step into leadership, not with anger or force, but with calm confidence.

That doesn't mean micromanaging. It means being clear, consistent, and present.

With Lucas, my previous riding horse, my relationship was different. We were together for more than ten years, and he trusted me implicitly. That deep trust allowed for more freedom. I could let him choose where to cross a stream or whether to trot or canter without needing to intervene. Because of the foundation we built, he felt secure in our partnership and trusted me to support him when he needed me.

Ben is still developing that confidence. When he's given too much freedom too soon, he starts to unravel. My job is to find the balance, offering him autonomy in small doses, but always with a steady presence.

In re-training him, we started with our "pre-flight" checks. Riding starts long before I get in the saddle; it starts on the ground. I assess his mood while grooming and tacking. Ben is tricky because he is stoic. Some horses show their emotions very easily, some do not. Ben does not, so his signals are subtle: tightness in his back, the way he holds his head, whether he zones out or tunes in. It takes an extra level of awareness on my part, of assessing where he is while grooming him. I check my own energy too. Am I nervous? Am I projecting worry? Horses can feel everything we bring to the relationship. If I carry anxiety into the saddle, he assumes there's something to fear and gets nervous.

When I am ready to mount up, I picture a good ride; I try to feel it. This is especially important with a spooky horse. For months I worked with him to stand still at the mounting block and not run off the second I got in the saddle. Something seemingly so small as keeping him still sets the stage for the ride. He needs to stand and relax and wait for me to get on calmly, and then he needs to stay there until I say it's time to go. Sometimes it's the small things we do to set the stage that make the most impact.

Approach and Retreat

On our first trail ride, I saw and felt firsthand what his previous owner had been facing. For most of the ride Ben seemed calm and steady, but the minute we turned towards home, he became a different horse. In the horse world, this is referred to as being "barn sour," meaning the horse wants to hurry up and get back to the barn. Since Ben was not the lead horse on most of the trail rides, he couldn't run toward home (because of the horses in front of him) unless we were in an open field, and then things got a little more tense. Ben is a very strong horse, so keeping him from taking off was a challenge.

If I rode Ben alone, I suspected it was not going to be a pleasant ride. I knew that he could "act up" out of insecurity and fear. I decided to try the training method of approach and retreat. We rode along the fence line of his pasture, where he felt safe. Then, little by little, we extended our rides, always returning to his "safe bubble" so he could regroup. I asked him to step toward the edge of his comfort zone, then retreat back to safety. The retreat had to come from me, not him. If I let him spin and run, he would be reacting, not learning. Instead, I needed to guide the process, to help him build new patterns. In this way, he could learn that discomfort can be temporary, and that I could lead him through it.

I believe in setting boundaries, for people and horses alike. But boundaries can be flexible. When we use them to keep ourselves safe, we sometimes make them so rigid that we stop growing. By gently pushing Ben's boundaries, without shattering them, I gave him space to adjust, to learn, to develop resilience.

Like a parent teaching a child to ride a bike; I'm the one keeping things steady and upright until that moment when the child has both the skill and confidence to go solo.

So, pilot or passenger?

In an airplane, most of us are happy to be passengers. But in relationships, especially with animals, children, or people who are learning to trust, we sometimes need to step into the pilot seat. Not out of control, but out of care. Ben has taught me that true leadership means listening as much as guiding. That we don't have to choose between rigid control and chaos, there's another way: calm clarity.

I'm grateful for everything he's teaching me. He's helped me refine my sense of timing, deepen my patience, and practice that delicate balance between stepping forward and stepping back.

Section I: Reflection Prompts

- Do some emotions affect you more deeply than others and make it harder to stay on track? Can you practice noticing them without being carried off by them?
- Think of a relationship where someone has started to withdraw. What role might your presence or expectations play?
- Can you think of times in your life when it is better to be the pilot and times when it is better to be the passenger?

SECTION II

My Favorite Classroom

This section provides a glimpse of the benefits of round pen work and some of the issues that can show up before we even touch a horse. This is where we turn the mirror to discover our truest self through the eyes of a horse.

The Round Pen

Like the famous book, *All I Really Need to Know I Learned in Kindergarten* by Robert Fulghum, many of the most valuable lessons I've learned in my life have been in the round pen. It is a magical place of understanding and learning.

The round pen is more than just a training tool; it's a place of connection, communication, and self-discovery. When I first started working in a round pen, I thought it was simply a way to instruct and train my horse. Over time I realized the depth of connection that was available to me, and I never again thought of the round pen as a training center, but as my favorite classroom. Working with horses at liberty helps us learn about ourselves in a fun and profound way. Here there is no hiding from the truth, if we are open to seeing and hearing it.

As I was training my first two horses, Ace and Cisco, I was introduced to round pen work by trainers who demonstrated amazing results with wild horses. At that time, I had no intention of ever turning this work into a business; I was simply exploring how to work with and build a partnership with my horses. I was discovering how to be a strong leader and uncovering new and better ways to communicate. My goals were to develop a meaningful relationship with my horses and to feel safe working with them and riding on trails.

Gradually, the insights I gained in the round pen began to spill over into my human relationships. I found myself applying the same principles of patience, clarity, and authenticity with my family, friends, and co-workers. Reflecting on past situations, I came to realize there were times I hadn't handled things as well as I could have.

I had an idea: what if I could take these lessons and structure a program that would allow people to come to my farm and gain insights through interactions with my horses? After the revelations of the Boy Scout visit, I decided to host more focus group gatherings and collect feedback from participants. I wanted to see if others experienced the same kind of breakthroughs I had, or if it was just me who found the horses so profoundly helpful.

The feedback was unanimous; everyone walked away with something meaningful from their time with the horses. The responses were overwhelmingly positive, often deeply personal, and spoke to real internal growth.

Through these sessions, I identified four core exercises, each one highlighting a different aspect of communication, which would form the foundation of the round pen classroom. In Section III of this book, I'll break down each of these exercises and share stories from actual clients who have participated in a session.

Before anyone steps into the round pen, I begin by working with a loose horse, with no ropes, halters, or tie-downs. This brief demonstration serves several purposes: it helps clients understand why they should trust me (by showing that I know what I'm doing), gives them a visual reference for what to expect, and allows me to introduce some of the common challenges they may face during their own sessions.

When a participant enters the round pen with me and the horse, we begin by simply allowing space for connection. The horse will often approach the participant to sniff and get a feel for the person's energy, and the participant usually needs a few moments to do the same, petting the horse, taking a breath, settling in. I explain the importance of this initial "meet and greet" by comparing it to human interactions.

Just as it's abrupt to launch into a conversation without a simple "good morning," it's inconsiderate to skip that first moment of connection with a horse. Taking the time to acknowledge each other sets the stage for a far more successful interaction.

The lessons learned in the round pen go far beyond horsemanship. They reveal how we communicate, how we connect, and how we lead. Horses teach us to be authentic. It is often a very humbling experience. Horses remain some of the best teachers I've ever known.

The Science

Most of the examples in this book are stories of actual client interactions with the horses. This section provides some research supported information, the science-backed benefits of being around and learning from horses. For years people have been studying horse/human interactions for mental health, emotional regulation and, more recently, leadership skills. Many studies have been conducted that conclude that being around horses can help reduce stress, anxiety and emotional dysregulation. Horses are highly sensitive, nonverbal animals that respond to human emotions and body language in real time. Feedback is immediate, which helps humans stay in the moment and quickly make adjustments. For many, feedback from horses (and animals in general) is easier to accept than feedback from humans. Horses have no ulterior motives, and they are without guile. This is why I say, "Horses don't play chess."

Often referred to as Equine Assisted Psychotherapy (EAP), or Hippotherapy, horses have been used to assist children with special needs such as autism, and veterans suffering from PTSD, and used as a supplement for other mental health treatments. A 2013 study from Washington State University found that children participating in equine-facilitated learning experienced lower levels of cortisol (the stress hormone) and demonstrated improved social competence and emotional awareness (Pendry and Roeter). More recently, an article titled *All About Equine-Assisted Psychotherapy* (PsychCentral 2022), identifies benefits such as enhanced confidence, emotional regulation, and improved social skills, while also reducing symptoms of anxiety, depression, trauma, and isolation.

From a neuroscience perspective, heart rate variability (HRV), a marker of stress and emotional regulation, has been shown to improve during horse-human interaction. In a collaboration between Dr. Ann Baldwin, Dr. Ellen Gehrke, and the HeartMath Institute, the energetic and physiological synchronization between horses and humans was studied. In this research, both human and horse participants were connected to EKG monitors while engaging in calm, intentional interaction. The findings showed that heart rhythms between the two species began to synchronize, indicating a measurable energetic coherence, a shared state of calm and connection. Horses' naturally strong electromagnetic heart fields appear to influence and regulate human heart rhythms, supporting the idea that horses help bring humans into physiological balance (Baldwin & Trent, 2018). This kind of synchronization not only enhances well-being, but supports emotional regulation, presence, and trust. There is a video on the HeartMath Institute website that summarizes the study (the link is in the reference section of this book).

Regarding leadership and the broader benefits of being around horses, author and researcher Linda Kohanov has written extensively on the subject, drawing from her decades of personal experience in equine-facilitated learning. Her books, including *The Power of the Herd* and *The Tao of Equus*, explore how horses help people cultivate emotional intelligence, authenticity, and relational presence. Kohanov describes horses as "nonpredatory teachers" because, unlike humans, they lead not through force, dominance, or verbal persuasion, but through clear intention, emotional congruence, and respectful awareness of others. Horses work best when those around them are honest and present in their communication, which helps individuals recognize and shift unconscious patterns in how they lead, connect, and respond. She introduces the concept of the "power of presence" as the ability to influence others through inner alignment; when thoughts, emotions, and actions are in sync. In this state, leaders become more grounded, responsive, and trustworthy, creating environments where others feel safe, seen, and motivated. Kohanov's work has been applied not only in personal growth settings, but also in training executives, educators, therapists, and military leaders, demonstrating the universal relevance of horse-based leadership lessons (Kohanov, 2013).

As with any form of coaching or therapy, the proof is found in the results. Does working with horses help people? Does it improve their physical well-being, enhance their communication, or make them better leaders? The answer is found in the stories of those who have experienced it firsthand. Throughout this book, and in my speaking engagements, I enjoy sharing the stories of clients who have participated in the Horse and People Project. I've also included a dedicated chapter at the end of this book where the voices and transformations of my clients are highlighted in their own words.

ASK LIKE YOU MEAN IT

There's No Crying in Horse Training

When I began learning to work with a horse in a round pen, I would trailer my gorgeous black and white paint, Cisco, to Ray, a local trainer. I was eager to learn from Ray because, while he understood natural horsemanship principles, he had developed his own methods from years of breaking, training, and teaching. We started with riding lessons, but it quickly became clear that Cisco and I needed groundwork in the round pen. The round pen exposed the holes in our relationship.

I vividly remember one particularly frustrating session. Cisco and I were both reaching our limits, and probably Ray was too. At one point, Cisco charged at me. I was horrified and frightened, overcome with frustration. I yelled at him, "I feed you, you should behave!" as if he owed me good behavior out of gratitude. I was on the verge of tears. Ray immediately kicked me out of the round pen. I felt like he was telling me, "There is no crying in horse training!"

I expected Ray to step in and discipline Cisco, to "teach him a lesson." Instead, Ray turned to me and began pointing out everything I was doing wrong. I was mortified. It was a humbling moment, and one for which I remain grateful.

Ray was right. As we continued working together week after week, he showed me how my inconsistencies and unclear cues were frustrating Cisco, sometimes even making him aggressive. I lacked confidence, and in the absence of clear leadership, Cisco would take advantage. One of the biggest lessons I learned was to stop blaming Cisco and accept that I had a part in creating our difficult relationship.

Yes, there were times when he was difficult. But the more I worked on myself, the better our relationship became. I realized I had been sending mixed signals and failing to set clear boundaries. I was ignoring problems hoping they'd resolve on their own; I had to address the behaviors I didn't like and take responsibility for my role in their nurturing. This was a profound lesson in boundary-setting and self-awareness. Until then, I hadn't noticed how often I let situations escalate until they became overwhelming. That's why Cisco seemed to go from 0 to 100 in a matter of seconds; I simply wasn't paying attention.

Before working with Ray, I had often considered selling or giving Cisco away. He felt too dangerous. Some of our trail rides were terrifying, when Cisco would transform into a galloping, bucking bronco. I remember one ride when a friend got angry at me for galloping off and scaring her horse. The truth was that I hadn't galloped off on purpose; Cisco had bolted, and I was desperately holding on. Cisco had turned toward home and decided he was getting there as fast as possible. By the time he finally tired, we ended the ride at a walk, but I was a trembling wreck in the saddle. Yet on other days, he would be an absolute angel, and I would regret ever considering parting with him.

Deep down, I knew that if I gave up on Cisco, I would really be giving up on myself.

Mirror, Mirror on the Wall

What if we all had a magic mirror that only told the truth? Would you want one? It depends on the circumstances, doesn't it?

Working with horses is like having a magic mirror. As I mentioned earlier, they are completely honest; they don't know how to lie.

If we think we're good communicators or effective leaders, horses will quickly reflect the truth. Horses don't care about our physical appearance, so we're free from the mirror's judgment on that front. What they care about is honesty, energy, integrity, consistency, clarity, and safety.

Some people embrace this reflection, grateful for the direct, unbiased feedback. Others struggle with it, realizing their perceived confidence or leadership isn't as solid as they thought. I've worked with individuals who initially resisted what the horse was showing them, only to have profound realizations later on. One woman, for example, came in believing she was assertive and in control. But when the horse ignored her cues, she discovered her energy was actually hesitant. The moment she stepped into a place of clarity and confidence; the horse responded immediately. She told me she had recently had surgery and was being careful with her movements. We spoke at length about the difference between being careful and being hesitant. There is a way you can behave in a careful manner, but your intention can still be clear and strong. She came into the pen a second time, and even though her movements were careful, her intention and body language was confident and the horse responded accordingly.

A few years ago, I held an open house for friends and family. In my effort to share the incredible teaching abilities of the horses, I invited guests to the farm and walked them through parts of the program. One visitor, Jessica, was a very kind, friendly, but quiet woman. She smiled the entire time and observed attentively until she was ready to volunteer and step into the round pen.

We talked and moved through the first few exercises with my horse, Ace. Everything was going smoothly, until it wasn't. At a certain point, Ace shut down. He would not approach Jessica, no matter what we tried. We worked at it for several minutes, but nothing changed. I couldn't understand what was happening, and I could see Jessica was close to tears. Despite her attempts to coax Ace, he simply wouldn't engage. Not wanting the situation to escalate in front of the group, I called for a 10-minute break, saying I thought Ace was tired.

I gently pulled Jessica aside and said, "The only time Ace won't approach me is when I'm putting on a brave face, but inside I'm really troubled." At that, Jessica began to cry. She admitted she had been smiling on the outside but was deeply unhappy inside due to some difficult life circumstances.

I explained that horses need authenticity. They don't understand when our energy doesn't match our expressions or actions. Smiling while radiating sadness made Ace uncomfortable, and he couldn't trust her.

With horses as my mirrors, I get to learn about myself in small increments. Then I go home, process what I've learned, and notice where those reflections show up in other areas of my life. Learning to be fully authentic comes with a degree of vulnerability, and that's not always easy to show.

Too Intense

One Saturday, a group of friends came out for a session. Everyone was enjoying the activities, and the energy was positive. We had Rocky in the round pen, and he was his usual mild-mannered, engaging self. Of all my horses, Rocky was always the most affectionate and calm. He had one blue eye, and one brown, a stocky frame and was two colors, chestnut (reddish) and white. A barn favorite because of his calm demeanor.

All the "meet and greets" went well, until Jonathan stepped into the pen. Rocky suddenly started running around and wouldn't stop. This was unusual behavior for him. When Jonathan asked what was going on, I replied, "You tell me. Rocky is picking up on something from you; he is not usually so animated."

With a wry smile, he admitted, "Well, people often tell me I'm too intense." Jonathan had come into the session determined to execute every exercise perfectly. He had watched his friends, mentally noting what worked and what didn't. He was so focused on getting everything right that he missed the subtleties of the interactions, the back-and-forth communication between horse and human. Jonathan did not see the question and answer, the turn of the head, the eye contact, the bend in the neck, the flick of the tail. Each movement had meaning, but Jonathan was too busy making his checklist to notice. His need for control cut off the interaction, making it one-sided.

This led to a discussion of real-life situations where we might skip the "meet and greet" and "getting to know you" aspects of interactions and what the impact was. How many of us have worked with managers who walk into the office with a rigid plan, issuing directives without engaging in dialog? How does that make us feel? Anxious? Nervous? Put off? Does it feel safe to ask questions or admit confusion when communication is only one-way? Leaders who don't encourage participation and interaction can unintentionally cause others to withdraw.

In the workplace, a top-down leadership or communication style can be effective in high-pressure or emergency situations. In day-to-day interactions, that same approach can come across as bossy, closed off, overbearing, standoffish, or even intimidating. The question is: do we want to be the kind of leaders, whether at work or at home, who cause our staff or families to shut down or hide?

In the round pen, approaching a horse with rigid, forceful energy often causes it to run away. So, what does that kind of energy do to the people around us? Humans may not bolt like a horse, but they have their own ways of running away. They might disengage, go silent, shut down emotionally, or withhold their best effort.

Another client, Sarah, a tall, quiet woman in her 60s, experienced a similar issue. When she entered the round pen, Rocky immediately started running. This time, I recognized Sarah's quiet intensity. I asked Sarah to relax and let go of her expectations. It didn't work. Then I noticed her tightly clenched hands.

"Relax your hands," I suggested. "Stretch your fingers and turn away from Rocky."

Bingo. The pressure lifted, and Rocky joined us in the center of the round pen. I deliberately shifted the mood, by chatting mindlessly with Sarah for a few minutes, allowing Rocky a chance to receive positive energy without expectations. This demonstrated the power of small adjustments, relaxation, softening, and connection.

Learning to step into the round pen with a horse without expectations is one of those tasks that sounds simple but is far from it. Both Jonathan and Sarah were quiet on the outside, but intense on the inside. They walked in full of expectations, thinking they had all the answers. They struggled to accept instruction, show uncertainty and vulnerability. True connection requires flexibility and openness.

In Jonathan's case, his team at work felt uneasy around him. They got nervous when he showed up, leading to poor productivity.

Like Rocky, they sensed the pressure and intensity. We talked about the importance of making connections. Just as Rocky needed a moment of casual interaction before work began, people need a sense of engagement. With a horse, that might be as simple as petting him and letting him smell you. With humans, like the members of Jonathan's team, it might mean asking about their day, their hobbies, or their families.

We spoke about engaging in small talk, but that was immediately met with resistance. Jonathan saw small talk as a waste of time and energy. But true efficiency comes from understanding people well enough to lead them effectively. How do you lead someone you know nothing about? People, like horses, respond to relationships built on trust, not just demands. Understanding strengths, weaknesses and abilities can only help you better encourage people in the right direction and be more efficient and effective in leading them.

It's Hard to Change!

Some people have been operating the same way for so many years, that it is hard for them to do things differently. I later found out that Sarah was a great communicator in her mind (aren't we all?) but the communication was often one-sided. She would write letters to relatives but not be concerned about receiving responses. There was never any feedback. She felt that because she was making the initial effort, this was all that was needed. If I treated my horses (or my children) like that, they would not want to spend any time with me.

Like the girl with the runaway horse, many horse people complain about not being able to catch their horses from the field. This is a problem with connection. They have established a relationship with that horse that is based only on the person's expectations and desires. There is no consideration for the horse.

Both Jonathan and Sarah did not want to "waste" time with the "trivial" things that help build connections. With horses (and humans), sometimes it is the small things that they appreciate. It may seem trivial to learn where they like to be scratched, where their favorite grazing spot is, what their favorite treats are, what makes them nervous, what makes them happy. However, the trust built from paying attention to these small details goes a long way.

At work, getting to know your colleagues personally can help create a more positive and collaborative environment. Many companies invest in team-building activities to encourage social interaction, with the goal of improving workplace culture. When people know each other beyond just job titles and tasks, trust increases and communication flows more easily.

This is true for leadership, too. When a boss takes the time to understand their employees, not just their roles, but their personalities, they can lead more effectively. Does this person need detailed instruction, or do they prefer to figure things out as they go? Are they visual learners, or do they absorb information best through written communication? Are they motivated by public recognition, or do they respond better to a quiet word of encouragement? Personalizing your leadership approach makes a difference; it can help employees feel valued, thereby increasing productivity.

In Mike Staver's, *Leadership Isn't for Cowards*, he describes good leadership as both a science and an art. The science is the technical side: getting the work done. But it's not just about the numbers. The art is in creating the right environment, where people feel supported and are set up to succeed. The artistic side is about culture: how to connect with team members, how to motivate them, and how to make space for their strengths.

When people feel heard, accepted, and valued, they perform better. The same is true for horses. That sense of being seen and respected, whether in the barn, the backyard, or the boardroom, matters. Think about how good it feels when the barista at your favorite coffee shop knows your order before you even say a word. Or when the waiter at your favorite restaurant remembers your name and preferences. These small, personal gestures make us feel known, and valued.

Participants have learned all these lessons without even touching a horse! Just by stepping into the round pen.

Content or Delivery?

There are many ways to share information, give directions, or ask questions. Often, it's how something is said that causes friction. When spoken harshly, judgmentally, or even just in a blunt, matter-of-fact way, words can rub people the wrong way. Think sandpaper.

Content and delivery are both essential elements of effective communication. Strong content educates, informs, persuades, adds value, and can entertain. However, poor delivery can cause the recipient to disregard it completely. Similarly, great delivery falls flat if the content is bad.

Anne is a friend whose elderly mother is being cared for by a healthcare provider. Anne spends as much time with her mother as possible; taking her to the store, out to eat, and on other little outings. Recently, the healthcare provider called a meeting, during which she laid out a list of rules about things Anne could and could not do with her own mother.

Can you imagine being told you're not allowed to take your 92-year-old mother out to lunch? Or saying that you cannot indulge your mother's joy in buying frozen vegetables? Not exactly a compassionate or effective approach.

The concern? Some of the mother's food purchases were making it difficult to maintain her necessary dietary restrictions. The content of the concern was understandable, but the delivery was terrible.

What if, instead, the health care provider had expressed her concerns and invited Anne into a conversation? Something like, "I've noticed some challenges with the diet we're trying to maintain. Can we work together to find a way for you to enjoy outings with your mom that also supports her daily routine?"

In this case, it wasn't the message that caused the upset; it was the delivery. It reminds me of how we work with horses. You can have the right intention and still get the wrong result if your energy, tone, or timing is off. Just like people, horses don't merely respond to what we ask; they respond to how we ask.

A few years ago, a friend adopted a horse from a local rescue. The horse is very sweet, but not especially brave, easily spooked, and nervous in unfamiliar situations. As my friend got to know him, she began learning the value of patience, softness, and steady leadership.

One of their early challenges came when trying to ride into the woods. Her horse was fine in the open field, but as they approached the tree line, he'd hesitate or refuse to go forward. The change in environment, from wide open space to a narrow, enclosed path, was too much for him.

My friend asked if she should carry a crop, which is a short stick often used to get the horse's attention or provide directional cues. Unfortunately, it can also be misused, sometimes becoming a tool of frustration rather than communication.

I wasn't sure how she intended to use it, so I advised her to avoid it. I explained that if she used the crop right at the edge of the woods, it could unintentionally reinforce the horse's fear. The very spot where he was already uncertain would then become the place where he felt punished. In that case, her delivery, even if her intent was only to encourage, could backfire and make things worse.

In moments like that, leadership is less about force and more about trust. I encouraged her to keep showing up calmly, confidently, and consistently. To give her horse time. To help him feel safe. Because whether we're dealing with horses or people, the message is only half the equation. How we deliver it, the tone, timing, and intention, can change everything.

Finding Neutral

Neutral is a place of calm, a reset point where everything settles. After a blow-up or high-stress situation, horses seek to restore peace. As prey animals, horses are highly sensitive and constantly on alert for danger. A simple rustling in the woods can trigger their instinct to think, "DANGER!" We cannot train that instinct out of them. They are quick to respond, which makes working with them challenging as well as rewarding.

We can help horses return to neutral. If we have built a foundation of trust and communication, a reassuring pat, or a calm, "It's okay," can go a long way. Our energy and body language are key; when we remain composed instead of reacting to their energy, they are more likely to mirror our state. It is a beautiful experience to help a 1,000-pound animal find neutral.

Just like horses, we all need ways to find neutral in our lives. We all seek a sense of safety, physically and emotionally. Studies show the damaging effects of chronic stress, making it essential to develop ways to release it. Humans tend to hold onto stress (and anger), while horses instinctively let it go.

Years ago, I offered riding lessons. One of the most common corrections I repeated to novice riders was to lower their hands. Posture is very important when riding, for balance, connection and leadership. When students would leave their hands up in the air instead of resting them lower near the horses' withers (shoulders), I would remind them to "find neutral" with hands lowered, a place of softness and relaxation.

At times, I would physically take the reins out of the client's hands and make them ride with their hands holding a strap attached to the saddle. This kept their hands in a more neutral position and helped relax their shoulders and torso. The students did not realize that by holding their hands in the air, they were inadvertently causing tension that then flowed to the horse, and then back to them, creating a tension loop.

One of the first corporate sessions I ran at Horse and People Project was for the staff of a restaurant. As anyone who's worked in the service industry knows, a restaurant is a high-stress environment, especially during peak hours. Tensions run high, with difficult issues like patrons, short staffing both in the kitchen and front of house, missing ingredients, and slow table turnover, to name a few. These challenges ebb and flow throughout a single shift, often without warning.

The question we focused on during their session was: How do you let the tension rise and fall without getting stuck in it, and without turning on each other?

Acknowledging that stress is inevitable, we focused on releasing tension, noting that holding onto it hurts not only the individual, but the whole team. At one point during the session, one of the horses let out a loud snort. The group burst out laughing. We talked about how snorting is a horse's way of releasing tension. It's a reset: simple, instinctive, and effective.

That led to a funny, yet meaningful conversation about whether people could "snort like a horse" at work to let go of stress. Snorting became a metaphor for the broader idea: treating tension as momentary, instead of carrying it around for the rest of a shift.

When you find a place of neutral, individually and as a team, you work better together. You make fewer mistakes. And you walk out the door with less weight on your shoulders. Life is full of stressful moments; we cannot avoid them. But watching how quickly horses transition from a heightened state to a place of neutrality has been a powerful lesson for me, and I often tell myself to try to "find neutral."

There have been times in my life when I could not "find neutral" and the horses reactions reflected my emotional state. When I was going through a separation and divorce, I often hid out in the barn with the horses. During those deep periods of depression, most of the horses gave me solace, except Ace. He would run away from me. At first, it made me even more depressed and a little angry. But slowly, I realized that Ace simply couldn't handle seeing me that low. He needed me to be strong for him.

Rocky, on the other hand, was a horse with a different gift. He would come to me, rest his head in my lap, and just be with me while I cried. When the tears stopped, I would take a deep breath and realize how much better I felt. Ace needed strength. Rocky helped me find it. This was a very spiritual and profound experience for me. I had to learn not to hold that difference against Ace, to accept the love and healing Rocky offered and love them both for who they were. Like people, different horses have different gifts, and Rocky's ability to help me return to neutral was a much-needed life raft.

Can't Stop Yawning

During a recent session, a group of five came as a birthday gift for one of the participants. One of them had been to the farm over a year ago, and it was inspiring to see how much progress they'd made since then.

As I was setting up, I paused to consider which horse to work with. Sometimes, I think of the group or the individual who is on their way and wonder which horse might offer what they need that day. I had Rocky in mind. I called his name, halter in hand, waiting by the gate. He began to make his way over…

But then Finn appeared. He flattened his ears at Rocky, his signal for Rocky to move aside. There was no question in Finn, no hesitation in his stride. Just a clear, wordless decision: It's me, today.

I've learned not to question, but to take the offering. Little did I know what an amazing experience we would have that day.

So, Finn it was. Finn is a gorgeous dark bay (brown) thoroughbred. He is tall and imposing, often skittish and nervous. I was surprised that he "volunteered" to participate in the session.

Everyone did great, and then it was time for the final participant, Helen, to step in. As is customary, we began by standing quietly together with the horse, allowing Finn to "meet" her.

In the center of the pen, our backs to the rest of the group, Finn stood quietly in front of us. And then, he yawned. A long, slow opening of the jaw and shake of the head. Then again. And again.

At first, I thought it was nothing, a simple release, maybe just tiredness. But the yawns kept coming. One after another, like waves rolling in. Six, seven, more. I lost count.

"This is unusual," I whispered. "He's never done this before." I was at a loss for how to explain it. Then, I turned to Helen. Her cheeks were wet with tears.

"I'm going to leave you alone for a moment," I said softly. "It seems there is a connection going on here that doesn't include me." She nodded, grateful. I stepped back, keeping my body between her and the rest of the group. Some moments are meant to be private, and this was one of them.

When she was ready to continue, she wiped her face and nodded at me. "Do you have any idea what that was about?" I asked.

"Yes," she said. "When I am overwhelmed, or anxious, I make myself yawn. It's how I soothe myself. It helps me to release pressure." She would usually use that method when she was in private, and she didn't want to do it while at the farm as part of a group.

To this day, I don't know how Finn knew. I don't know why he picked up on the thread and carried it for her. Sometimes the experiences with the horses are truly spiritual. Sometimes what happens in the round pen reaches far beyond what we can explain.

Section II: Reflection Prompts

- Think of a time when you felt overwhelmed or rejected in a leadership or parenting moment. Was there anything about that situation that could have been different?
- Do people stop talking when you enter a room? Are you aware of the energy that you carry?
- What is your version of the snort, or yawn? Do you have a simple habit or practice that helps you release stress and find neutral?

SECTION III

Round Pen Sessions

The round pen sessions comprise the heart of the Horse and People Project. Here we walk through the four key exercises, each highlighting a distinct and essential piece of the communication puzzle.

ROUND PEN SESSIONS SECTION III

EXERCISE 1: The Back-Up

In a herd, the lead horse is the one who controls the movement, the feet, of the others. A simple pin of the ears or a shake of the head can be enough to make another horse back off or move away. With our first exercise, The Back-Up, we mimic this kind of leadership by asking a horse to back up a few steps, which helps establish our role as the leader.

This exercise establishes leadership and clarifies who's in charge. It helps each individual find their unique balance between firmness and softness, using the horse's honest feedback as a guide. The focus is on energy, intention, presence, and the ability to lead with clarity, not force.

The exercise goes like this: each participant states out loud how many steps they want the horse to take, usually two or three, though occasionally someone wants to challenge themselves and goes for five or six steps. The actual method for asking the horse to back up varies. It can be as subtle as directing energy toward the horse, or more physical, like placing a hand on the horse's chest or face and applying pressure until the horse steps back. The key is that the amount of pressure used should be tailored to each horse-human interaction.

Some people come on too strong, and we work on softening their approach. Others are hesitant; they push or prod, but without real intention, and the horse may not respond at all. This lesson becomes a mirror for our intention, energy and clarity. Most horses will not respond to a purely physical approach. It is important to start with intention and energy and follow up with physical touch.

I always ask participants to say the number of steps out loud. If they don't, they often end up pushing without purpose, thinking the goal is simply to get the horse to move. But the real aim of the lesson is to be intentional and precise. If you ask for three steps, that's all you should get. Sometimes people get "bonus" steps and are thrilled, but I use that moment to point out that those extra steps may not be a sign of leadership. Often, it just means the horse was avoiding the person. There's no clarity, no focus. Avoidance is not good leadership.

So, the rule is simple: Ask for two steps? Get two steps. Start pressure, release pressure. That's the rhythm. Sounds simple, right? But it's deceptively so. The clarity it demands from us reveals just how vague we often are and how hard it is for humans to ask with intention and then to release pressure.

Releasing Pressure

In the horse world, releasing pressure can be as simple as softening your focus and not looking directly at the horse. Pressure isn't always physical; it can be energetic. Horses are much more sensitive to energetic pressure than most humans, and they can help us learn about the energy we carry. A glance, a touch, and even our presence carries an expectation. When we look away or turn around, we release that expectation, giving the horse space to process and respond.

When I ask a horse to move and he takes a single step, the most important moment is what I do next. If I immediately take my eyes off him or relax my body, I've told him yes, that was the right answer. The release is the reward.

In the human world, the same principle applies. We are often full of expectations, of how someone should act, respond, or agree with us. Releasing pressure here can mean letting go of those expectations. This might look like walking away, choosing not to push the point, or dropping the argument altogether.

Imagine having a heated conversation with a colleague, a spouse, or even a child. Sometimes the wisest move isn't to add more words or push harder; it's to step back, release the tension, and give the other person room to come forward on their own.

We should not expect the people in our lives to read our minds; we should not expect the horse to either. We must be clear, consistent, and intentional if we want to achieve our goals. Humans are notorious for giving vague instructions and then expecting perfect follow-through.

In the round pen, we never move on to the next lesson until this one is solid. The horses are endlessly patient, working with each person until they get it right. I always demonstrate a few different ways to ask for a back-up, whether it's pushing the air in front of the horse, applying a light nudge to the horse's nose, or pressing gently on the horse's chest. Each participant then gets to try it for themselves and see what works in their own interaction with the horse.

This lesson goes far beyond the round pen. It reminds us that true leadership isn't about control; it's about clarity. It's about having a clear ask, matching our energy to that intention, and knowing when to release. When we're clear within ourselves, others (horse or human) can understand and respond. When we're ambiguous, we invite confusion. The beauty of this exercise is that it brings our internal state to the surface, where we can work with it.

With a horse as our guide, we begin to understand how much more powerful we are when we lead with focus, not force.

Where Is Your Energy Going?

When Rocio came for her session, she was struggling to get Ace to back up. Ace, an extremely sensitive horse, usually responded to the slightest cue. Rocio kept throwing her hands outward, pushing air to the left and right. Ace stood still, unmoved. Rocio looked at me, confused.

I asked her, "Where are you directing the energy from your hands? Why are you sending it to the sides when he's standing right in front of you?"

The moment she redirected her energy and her gestures, and faced him directly, Ace immediately backed up.

It clicked. In that instant, Rocio had a breakthrough.

Rocio is a middle school teacher, and she'd been having trouble getting her students to turn in their assignments. She was caught between not wanting to hold their hands through every step of every assignment, while also not wanting to leave them completely on their own to manage deadlines. Something in her approach wasn't working.

The lesson from Ace was simple but powerful: she hadn't been directly engaging with her students. Instead, she was talking around them; her energy was directed towards the room, not the students. Phrases like, "Are we all getting the homework done?" or "Does everyone understand the assignment?" lacked the clarity and personal connection her students needed.

From this small but mighty moment in the round pen, she realized she needed a new way to reach her students, one that didn't embarrass them or call them out for having questions, but still made them feel seen and heard. One idea was to break the class into small groups and spend a few minutes with each group, checking in, answering questions, and engaging with them in a more focused, personal way. Ace helped Rocio find a clearer path to connecting with her students.

So often in life, we think we're being clear because we're saying the right things. But our energy, our direction, our presence, that's what people and animals respond to. You can say all the right words to someone, but if you're not truly connected, they won't feel it, just like Ace didn't.

Whether we're teaching students, leading teams, parenting children, or navigating relationships, the lesson holds: clarity requires connection. Not forceful, not loud, but intentional and honest. Sometimes, all it takes is one horse, one moment, to remind us how to get back on track.

You Can't Make Me

"Why isn't he moving?" Jake asked, clearly frustrated.

"Because he knows you don't want to be here," I replied.

This happened during a session when a group of moms brought their teenage sons to the farm. The other young men had gone through their turns in the round pen with interest and ease, but when it came time for Jake, Ace wouldn't budge.

"My mom forced me to come. I don't want to be here," Jake said.

I nodded. "I get that, and I'm sorry. But how about we leave Mom out there, and you be here with Ace? Just give him your attention. Let's see what happens."

You can probably guess what happened next. The moment Jake made the choice to try—really try—everything changed. His energy shifted, and Ace responded immediately. What began as a difficult, resistant session transformed into a surprisingly beautiful connection.

It was such a clear reminder: when we approach something half-heartedly, the results are often just as lackluster. Horses are remarkable in this way; they call us out on our mediocrity. Without judgment, without words, they reflect our presence, or lack of it. It's humbling and exhilarating.

With horses, you can't lie about your intentions. You can't fake your motivation. And they won't pretend along with you to help you save face. They meet you exactly where you are. We have to leave our egos behind and accept the teaching they offer.

As humans, we are often more perceptive than we'd like to acknowledge. Think about a time when someone completed a task, but you could tell their heart wasn't in it. The energy was off, even if the action was technically completed. Now flip that around and think of a time you gave that same kind of "just going through the motions" energy to something. Odds are, the person on the receiving end noticed. The work was accomplished, and sometimes that is enough, but other times the energy just feels off and the result is blah.

In work, in relationships, in life, you get what you give. We can't give 50% and expect to receive 100% in return. The lesson Jake learned that day, with Ace's help, was about the power of choosing to show up fully. To try. To be present.

Split Energy

A few months ago, I was giving a presentation at a local Rotary Club. The room was full of business owners, community leaders, and parents. People who, much like me, wear many hats. Besides having individuals and groups out to the barn, I also enjoy public speaking, taking the stories and lessons on the road, just like the ones in this book.

As I shared a story about one of my clients who was struggling with intention and clarity, I noticed the curious looks in the audience. They weren't quite sure how this challenge would connect to working with horses. That's often the case until I share both sides of the story: the horse's response and the human lesson behind it.

The story went like this: my client, Jane, was in the round pen, getting ready to ask my horse, Ace, to back up. Instead of applying gentle pressure and walking toward him with purpose, she pushed at him with her hands, while the rest of her body moved backwards. Her hands said forward, but her body said backward. Then she wondered why Ace wouldn't respond; he just stood there.

I asked Jane to pause and notice where her energy was going. Was it forward or backward? The answer was both. She was split down the middle, giving Ace two messages at once. No wonder he froze. The moment she took a breath, composed herself, aligned her intention with her movement, and brought her whole body into her ask, Ace backed up immediately. The follow-through was crucial, as it often is. Setting the intention clearly in her mind was the first step.

As I acted this moment out during my Rotary talk, using my body to demonstrate Jane's push-pull energy, the audience nodded in recognition. They could see how the physical direction could be misleading or confusing.

Then I had my own realization: I had been doing the very same thing in my life. My days were filled with too many commitments, family responsibilities, writing deadlines, speaking opportunities, and farm work. I felt like I was pulled in ten different directions, and as a result, nothing was moving forward. Talk about split energy!

It was such a powerful moment for me. It was a reminder that focus isn't just mental; it's physical, emotional, and energetic. Horses feel it immediately, but people feel it too. When we scatter ourselves, we confuse others and stall our own progress. But when we align all parts of ourselves, our intention, our actions, our bodies, our voices, we find clarity and can move forward.

EXERCISE 2: The Send

Humans share a universal fascination with watching horses run. Observing their movement; fluid, powerful, and free, evokes a sense of awe. For participants in our sessions, being the one responsible for initiating that movement often leads to feelings of empowerment and control. It can be exhilarating to send a thousand-pound animal into motion with just the shift of your intention, your body, or a flick of the line attached to the training stick we often use during sessions.

This exercise is about timing, patience, listening, feedback and trust. Effective communication is more than just speaking. It involves listening, pausing, reflecting, having physical and emotional boundaries and responding with clarity and consistency.

I always remind participants that while it is enjoyable to initiate speed and motion, the deeper value lies in being able to draw the horse back towards us. In other words, the real work, the true connection, is not in sending the horse away, but in inviting him to return. The magic is in the draw, not the send.

As prey animals, horses are wired to move away from pressure, from energy, from anything that feels uncertain or threatening. As discussed in a previous chapter, flight is their first and only instinct. Humans have fight or flight instincts. This is what makes it possible for firefighters to go into burning buildings. We can assess situations and act accordingly.

Horses simply run. Because of this, it is relatively easy to send a horse away; even a beginner can create enough pressure to cause a horse to move. But bringing them back, inviting them in, that's where trust shows up. That's where the relationship deepens. Again, this cannot be faked.

After we've practiced the first exercise, asking the horse to yield and take a few steps back, we move on to asking for motion. The first exercise lays the foundation for more advanced communication. In the second exercise, The Send, we ask the horse to move out and around us, following the curve of the round pen. The horse is encouraged to move along the fence line and maintain that motion until asked to return. Participants must find a balance between applying enough pressure to initiate movement and knowing when and how to release that pressure to signal the invitation to come back. The horse will often "ask" to return; he will keep an eye and an ear trained on us in the middle of the pen as a way to "listen" for when we are ready to receive him.

Here is where the deeper work begins. The dance between sending and drawing often reveals far more than words ever could. It sounds simple, but this is often where deeper behavior patterns begin to surface. Finding that balance between sending and drawing, or what I call the push/pull balance, tends to shine a light on how individuals lead and relate to others, and where they get stuck.

This is where the micromanagers show up, where the ineffective leaders stumble, and where the most guarded individuals have trouble connecting. Common personal tendencies begin to emerge. Participants who struggle with control may become overly focused on managing every step the horse takes, micromanaging rather than guiding. They spend so much time chasing and sending that the horse does not want to return. The balance is off.

Other participants, who are unsure or lack confidence in their communication, may have difficulty getting the horse to respond at all. Those who are emotionally guarded often face the greatest challenge when it comes time to invite the horse back in, because doing so requires openness, vulnerability, and trust. It's an act of partnership, not dominance.

Lead from Behind

We've all heard sayings such as "lead by example" and "a good leader shows the way," but what about "lead from behind"?

When I first started working on The Send exercise with my horse Cisco, he would constantly and abruptly stop and change direction. It was very frustrating, and I didn't understand why he was doing that; of course, I thought Cisco was in the wrong. Why didn't he understand my instructions? I was mimicking what I watched other trainers do, or so I thought. I took this issue to my trainer, who easily diagnosed that I was cutting Cisco off, so he had no option but to turn. Cisco was doing exactly what I was asking for. I was the one that was in the wrong. My trainer told me I was blocking Cisco.

"How can that be? I'm not anywhere near him!" I insisted defensively.

"It's where you are standing in relation to his body. You are putting pressure on his shoulder, and that inadvertently blocks him, so he has nowhere else to go," the trainer replied. This was when I started really understanding how much pressure we can apply energetically, without any physical touch.

A horse's power comes from their hind end. If you watch a racehorse, they generate power by pushing from their back legs, while their front legs are catching them. Like many four-legged animals, they are rear-wheel-drive machines. There is a reason that farmers herd their sheep from behind, and cowboys herd cows from the rear. There may be a lead horse showing the way, but most of the herding is done by applying pressure from behind.

Similarly, when in their own herds, the lead horse is usually the one in the rear, pushing rather than pulling, leading from behind. As humans, and predators, we tend to be in front, dragging rather than supporting.

When I began working with the horses in the round pen, I had to learn how to lead from behind. To apply pressure on a horse's back end to cause forward motion. I had to learn not to drag them around by their heads. Standing in front of them leaves them nowhere to go but back; it blocks their movement. By remaining near their back end, I give them all of the space and opportunity required to allow them to proceed forward.

What does this have to do with communication and leadership? As humans, we're a little too used to dragging people around, rather than encouraging and leading from behind. Instead, can we learn to plant an idea and give people space to see what they do with it? Can we learn not to micromanage? Leading people "from behind" also allows for some individuality, the freedom to choose their own path, and to be creative with the process. If you give people the general idea of a desired outcome and encourage them "from behind," you might be pleasantly surprised by the results.

Is Anybody Listening?

Josie came to me as a stay-at-home mom with two young children, ages eight and five. She felt unheard in her household. When she said "No," no one listened, and worse, when she tried to lead, instruct, or direct the kids, they would often throw tantrums. Josie had taken a break from her career in sales to raise her children. She was accustomed to working in a high-energy environment with lots of autonomy and client interaction. In sales, she had learned to handle rejection, which fueled her passion to win over clients. But at home, it was an entirely different story.

Josie's session started off well. We took our time standing and petting Ace and then moved onto the first exercise of backing him up. She had no issues. Then we moved onto the send exercise. Josie had no problem sending Ace out, and I told her it was up to her to decide when to invite Ace back in. She could invite him back in at any moment or keep him out on the fence line until she was ready. At one point, Ace looked over, clearly asking if he could approach, and Josie said, "No, not yet." Ace stopped in his tracks and waited patiently.

Josie was amazed.

"Let's do that again!" she said, so we did. She sent Ace out on the rail, and once more, when Ace asked to come back, she said "No," and he kept going. Josie was so moved, nearly in tears, and said, "I feel heard!" Directing a 1,000-pound animal without a fight is incredibly powerful and empowering.

The third time, I suggested she allow Ace to approach her. I explained, "If you say 'No' all the time, you risk creating a dynamic of constant resistance, pushing him away rather than fostering connection." By letting Ace approach, I assured Josie, she could still maintain authority. She was able to monitor his speed and set clear boundaries, without losing control. Clear boundary-setting and making her words matter was key for Josie in this exercise.

Josie shared a specific situation at home: when she was preparing dinner, the kids would be playing, and when she announced that dinner was ready, they had a hard time disengaging from their games and coming to the table. This often led to heightened emotions and tantrums. Josie felt like the bearer of bad news, interrupting their fun, making her the target of their unhappiness. We talked about how to soften this interaction.

Timing is everything. This statement, while true for humans, is even more important when working with horses, almost as important as the instruction itself. During our session with Ace, when we asked for a movement, we gave him a grace period to accomplish the task. If we asked him to stop, we allowed him a few extra steps, as it's hard for a horse to stop abruptly unless trained to do so. Young children also need time to transition from one activity to another. Announcing, "Times up!" without warning made it hard for Josie's children to adjust.

Josie asked me: how could she carry her success in the round pen with a horse to her interactions at home with her young children? We brainstormed a few strategies to specifically address the dinnertime meltdowns:

- Set a timer for 10-15 minutes to give the kids a warning, so they can begin cleaning up.
- Have the older child set the timer. It would make him feel responsible and provide a sense of ownership.
- Have the younger child turn off the timer, helping her feel part of the process, again making her less likely to resist.
- Trial and error. If one solution doesn't work, try something else.
- Flexibility and negotiation go a long way.

There is no single "right" answer. A friend suggested giving a child two options and letting the child choose between the two. That gives the adult some control, yet the child makes the final decision and feels like they have some control as well.

As kids get older, they can become more involved in decision-making. You can ask, "How would you like this to go?" Finding a win-win for both sides and protecting your relationship with your kids is key.

This same interaction can be seen in an office setting. Starting with an end goal in mind, allowing for input, flexibility and negotiation about the process can go a long way in accomplishing goals and helping individuals feel they have some ownership and responsibility for the outcome.

My Daughter's Tattoo

When my daughter turned 16, she announced she wanted a tattoo.

Caught off guard, I immediately said, "No!" She countered with, "Well, I have a friend who tattoos in his basement. I could just go there, and you'd never know."

I didn't fundamentally have a problem with tattoos, but she was only 16. I felt she was too young to make such a permanent decision. Teenagers often believe they know themselves completely and telling them otherwise doesn't always go well. Tattoos are both permanent and painful, and I wasn't sure she was ready to make a choice she might later regret.

She was determined, however, and the thought of her going to a high school classmate's basement for permanent ink was alarming. We went back and forth, both holding our ground. We were at a standstill. The situation reminded me of when I was retraining Ace shortly after adopting him. He had been bred to race but did not do well on the track and was discarded. I adopted him from a rescue organization and planned to use him as a pleasure riding horse.

While working with Ace in the round pen, he would occasionally get stuck, literally. He would plant his feet and refuse to move. My experience with the Back-Up exercise taught me that I should not be the one moving back. If Ace refused to move and I stepped back first, I would inadvertently confirm that he was the leader. However, if neither of us moved, we were simply stuck, our communication cut off entirely.

After standing and staring at each other for a while, I realized I could move *sideways*, rather than backward, to get him to shift. The sideways movement wasn't perceived as a retreat, but as a way to change the course of our interaction without engaging in a battle of wills. This lesson: *redirect rather than retreat*, became invaluable not only in training but in parenting, and in leadership in general.

Faced with my daughter's tattoo request, I realized I had to figure out how to get us unstuck. If I simply said yes, would she see it as a retreat? Would I set a precedent that she (and her siblings) could always wear me down? Maybe. But if I stayed firm in my "no," it could lead to constant resistance, and I risked pushing her into a risky decision. Ultimately, she was leaving the door open for discussion, and it was up to me whether I left it open or slammed it shut.

I saw two choices:

Choice #1: Stick to my "no" and shut down any conversation about tattoos. The possible outcomes? She might obey me but harbor resentment, or she might go ahead and get the tattoo behind my back. Then what could I do? Punish her? Take away her phone? Ground her? Would this lead to more secrecy, sneaking out, and a relationship built on dishonesty and resentment? I knew that wasn't the kind of relationship I wanted with my daughter. I loved my mother, but we weren't close when I was growing up. She wasn't someone I confided in or sought advice from. This path didn't feel right.

Choice #2: Reconsider, redirect, and negotiate. Could we discuss my concerns regarding hygiene, permanence, changing tastes, and find a compromise? At 16, teenagers crave autonomy. Silencing their voices doesn't foster a strong future relationship.

I realized, just like with Ace, that I needed to make the first move. I was the parent. I was the adult. I needed to guide this moment constructively keeping in mind that the relationship was more important than the conflict.

So, we negotiated. I agreed she could get a tattoo; she would pick the design and placement with my approval (no skull and crossbones). In return, I would select the tattoo studio and cover the cost. Tattoos are expensive, so this seemed like a fair compromise. Plus, I got to be there with her. In many ways, tattooing today feels like the new ear piercing, and a mother-daughter rite of passage. I was thankful to be included in the experience.

Did this mean we never had another conflict? Of course not. But it was a pivotal moment of growth. And the only precedent it set was that I would strive to redirect, negotiate, and keep communication open with all my children as they grew.

The Big Boss

Another day, another session. This time, it was a company outing, with about twenty employees, including staff, managers, and the boss himself. From the moment they stepped out of their cars, I could tell this was not a voluntary retreat. Many of the employees stood around with their arms folded, their expressions set in quiet resistance. The atmosphere was heavy, and I could feel the tension in the air. This was meant to be a team bonding experience, but I wasn't sure the team wanted to bond at all. I always feel extra pressure when I feel my audience is resistant. Will the participants be open to what the horses teach?

As always, the horses had their own way of working their magic. Slowly, the barrier between the people and the experience began to soften. Conversations started, and laughter bubbled up. The horses were already weaving a quiet connection, pulling people in, lightening the energy of the morning. And being in nature on a beautiful sunny day didn't hurt.

That is, until the big boss entered the pen.

He strode in with a dominant energy that was hard to miss. I could almost hear his thoughts: "I'm going to show this horse who's in charge!" He told me he had plenty of experience with horses and was not at all concerned about taking his turn in the round pen. His stance was forceful, his eyes locked on Ace; I wasn't sure if he wanted to teach Ace or his employees a lesson, or both.

Sure enough, he pushed. He prodded. He used force, even intimidating Ace to the point where the horse refused to return to the center of the pen where we were standing. Ace stayed at the far end, his body tense and wary, clearly feeling the pressure. Ace even threw a kick in the direction of the boss. We were many feet away, so there was no real danger of getting kicked; it was just Ace's way of showing displeasure.

"He just gave you the finger," I said, which led to the group breaking out in laughter. I had hoped that by pointing that out, the Boss would understand that his energy and instruction were not being well received by Ace. When the boss finally released the pressure and asked Ace to join him in the middle of the pen, Ace would not approach.

"Why won't he come back in for me like he did for everyone else?" the boss asked me.

"You just spent the last ten minutes chasing him away," I said gently. "Why do you think he'd want to come back to you now?"

I had warned him about the dangers of constantly sending, of pushing too hard. But he wouldn't listen. He had created a situation in which Ace did not feel safe. Sometimes I have to let people experience the consequences of their own actions. Only then can they begin to understand that there's a better way.

This day happened to bring me a particularly stubborn client. He didn't see anything wrong with what he was doing, and was not open to my guidance. He wasn't ready to fail, not in front of his team. We stumbled through the session, and ultimately got Ace to approach, but with resistance.

Afterwards, I pulled one of the managers aside. I had a feeling about the underlying dynamics of the group. "Do you have an issue with employee turnover?" I asked, watching her reaction closely.

Her eyes widened, and she replied, "Yes! How did you know?"

It was clear to me, and to Ace, that the boss was a classic top-down leader, one who took no feedback, and who made it clear that control was his priority. When employees feel unable to voice their concerns, or when they're constantly micromanaged, the workplace becomes suffocating.

During the session, I had repeatedly said to the boss, "He's already going. You don't need to keep after him." Ace was doing exactly what was being asked, but the pressure never let up. It was as if the boss couldn't stop himself from pushing, from making sure every step was exactly how he wanted it.

At one point, the boss turned to me, seeking validation, or perhaps just an answer.

"What would you say my leadership style is?" he asked, eyes searching mine for a hint of approval.

The staff around us seemed to hold their collective breath, waiting for my response. I had to be careful with my words. After all, the people he led were listening.

Instead of labeling him a micromanager, I chose my words carefully. "I think you probably hover more than you need to."

He blinked, the truth settling in for a moment. "But I need to make sure everyone is doing their job," he replied, justifying his constant vigilance.

"If you hire the right people for the right job," I said, my voice steady, "you shouldn't have to hover. Maybe the issue isn't with them, maybe it's with your hiring process."

There was a long pause. He didn't respond right away. And the session carried on, with little change in his approach.

I'd love to say that this boss took the feedback to heart and made meaningful changes, but the truth is, I'm not sure he did. Some lessons, it seems, are harder to learn than others, and some people are harder to teach than others. The horses offer the lessons, but it is up to us to accept and apply the changes in our lives.

There is also a lesson within a lesson here. Do micromanagers get a bad rap? Does micromanaging create more problems than it solves? High turnover means constant training and less time for work. But it may be too easy to label a seemingly domineering boss as a micromanager. The truth may be that they are forced to manage individuals who are not well-suited for their jobs. Either way, corporate policies may require further evaluation.

Lick and Chew (Couples Therapy!)

Horses do a funny thing as part of their communication: they lick their lips and make chewing motions with their jaws. It might look like they're just casually mouthing something or relaxing, but this small gesture is a powerful signal. It usually follows a moment of pressure, learning, or internal processing. While humans might nod or say, "Got it," horses respond by licking and chewing. It's their way of showing they've understood and accepted or let go of something.

I often tell clients, "Wait for his lick and chew," as a reminder to slow down. It's not just about giving the horse time to respond; it's about honoring that a conversation is taking place, even when it's silent. We can't keep talking, keep asking, keep pushing, and expect connection. We need to wait for a response.

During a couple's session, one of the wives came into the round pen to work with Rocky. From the numerous stories in this book involving Rocky, you can probably tell he was a special horse. Honest and responsive, slow to anger and quick to accept. During the Send exercise, the wife kept escalating the pressure, asking Rocky to move more, turn tighter, and yield quicker, even though he was already doing exactly what she'd asked for. It was not subtle; she couldn't quite let go of the pressure no matter how many times I said, "Wait for his lick and chew!" She had trouble recognizing when enough was enough.

This is a common place where people get stuck: the transition between asking and allowing. Between encouraging, and (let's be honest) nagging. I gently reminded her again and again, "Wait for the lick and chew!" I was trying to help her to pause, breathe, and let the conversation settle.

"Is Rocky doing what you asked of him?" I asked.

"Yes, he sure is" she responded.

"Then why do you keep the pressure on? Why not back off and let him go?" I asked. "Are you waiting for his lick and chew?" Suddenly, her husband, who'd been watching quietly, jumped out of his seat and blurted out,

"Yeah, you have to wait for MY lick and chew!"

We all cracked up. It was a perfect moment of humor, but also clarity. The whole dynamic they'd been caught in came into focus in that one sentence. I love when the connections are made in real time, and the lesson from the horse can be correlated to real-life situations.

"Keep in mind that you're both right," I offered once the laughter settled. The wife didn't want to come off as a nag (who does?), and the husband didn't want to feel nagged. But the breakdown wasn't about tone or intent, it was about timing and acknowledgment. He wasn't giving her any signal that he'd heard her, so she kept repeating herself, trying to get a response. And the more she repeated herself, the more he shut down. I think we've all been caught in this classic loop.

"Could the solution be as simple as the husband saying, "I'm processing," or "I hear you, let me think about it and get back to you?" I asked. That tiny bit of feedback, his version of a lick and chew, might be all it takes to shift the pattern. He would get space, she would feel heard, and the pressure could be released.

It's amazing how often the lessons in the round pen mirror the ones outside of it. Whether it's with horses or humans, communication isn't just about what's said or done, it's about the space in between. That's were working with horses can help us learn about ourselves, and how our actions either help or hinder situations. How many of us can learn to be patient and "wait for the lick and chew"?

Too Noisy

Noise isn't just about volume or sound. It can show up in our bodies, our thoughts, even in the subtle tension we carry without realizing it. Horses are masters at picking up on all of it. They notice the things we gloss over, the gestures we repeat unconsciously, the energy we bring into a space. Working with them often reveals how much "noise" we carry into the conversation without ever saying a word. One of my favorite authors, Eckhart Tolle, says that the biggest noisemaker in our lives is not the TV or phone, it's our own mind. Horses have the uncanny ability to pick up when our minds (and bodies) are being noisy. We give off a different energy when we are being noisy.

I was reminded of this during a round pen session with a client. We were working with Ace, who usually loved to engage. But that day, for some reason, he wouldn't approach. We gave him space, invited him in, and softened our energy to release any pressure, but he just stood there, watching us from about 20 feet away. He was alert, but unmoving.

I stood quietly, observing both horse and human, when I noticed something. My client, wanting so badly for Ace to come in, was unknowingly moving his hands over and over in a subtle "come here" motion. His intention was soft, but his body was speaking a different language, one that might have felt confusing or even insistent to the horse.

I gently asked him to bring his hands to stillness. To stand, breathe, and simply be present. Within seconds of the change, Ace flicked an ear, lowered his head slightly, and took a step toward us. Then another, until he was standing in front of my client.

It was such a small shift, my client quieting his hands, but the impact was immediate.

To Ace, those repeated hand movements were probably like visual static, constant, low-level noise that disrupted the invitation. His response was to stand still and not approach. Instead of blaming him, we needed to figure out why he was keeping away.

We often limit our idea of "noise" to what we hear, but in the horse world, noise can be anything: excessive movement, anxious energy, or even the internal pressure we put on ourselves to make something happen. Horses feel all of it.

That moment reminded me how powerful it is to get quiet, truly quiet, not just in our voices, but in our bodies, our energy, our intentions. When we settle ourselves, we make space for true connection. We create an atmosphere where a horse can feel safe enough to approach.

I've learned to make a conscious effort to notice when I'm being noisy, even if I don't think I am. It's not my job to fill every silence with sound or motion. In fact, some of the richest moments come from stillness. It's not always easy to hold that kind of quiet, especially in a world that teaches us to always be doing something, to fill every moment with activity. The horses are patient teachers. They show us, again and again, how to soften, settle, and be quiet. This continues to be one of the hardest lessons for me personally.

ROUND PEN SESSIONS — SECTION III

EXERCISE 3: The Leg

Asking a horse to give up its leg is a big deal. As previously mentioned, horses are prey animals; they rely on their ability to run from danger. When we take away their ability to flee, even momentarily, it requires a high level of trust.

The mantra "Ask Like You Mean It" was born from this exercise, asking the horse to yield his leg. What seems like a simple request is actually a powerful lesson. It's not about demanding; it's about meaning what you ask for, and standing behind it with calm, confident energy. This exercise reveals how often we hesitate, second-guess ourselves, or send mixed messages.

It's always fascinating to watch how my horses respond to different individuals. Who will a horse release his leg to, and who won't he release it to? Some people need a lot of coaching through this exercise, while others seem to manage it naturally. I often wonder: how does this experience reflect their lives outside the ring? Are they clear when they ask for things? Are they fair? Do they feel safe to others?

Horses have powerful instincts and make split-second decisions. I can't force a horse to give up his leg to someone if he's not willing. That willingness has to come from the horse, and it usually does. We always complete the exercise; it's just a matter of time and guidance. Once we've made the request, we cannot back down until we've succeeded. We just need to find the right balance, the right approach for everyone.

Some individuals stand too close, others too far. Some are too rough or demanding; others are overly gentle or hesitant. The key is finding that balance of firm, yet safe.

Ask Like You Mean It

A few years ago, I invited one of my sisters to my house for a BBQ. At the end of the invitation, I said, "I know you are really busy, so don't worry if you can't come."

"So, am I invited or not?" she asked, followed by, "The way you worded that invitation makes it sound like you don't really want me to come, you were very quick to give me an excuse not to be there." I was surprised by her response; of course I wanted my sister to come to my BBQ!

This interaction made me think a lot about how we ask for things. Why do we feel the need to help others with their responses? I didn't want my sister to feel bad if she couldn't come, so I wanted her to know I wouldn't be upset. Why was I hesitant to let her decide and answer for herself?

The better invitation would have been, "I'm having a BBQ, and I'd love for you to come." Her response mostly likely would have been, "Thank you for the invitation. I'm not sure I can be there, but I'll try my best!"

During a session at the barn, Olivia struggled to get through the leg lifting exercise. She poked, prodded, tapped, and pulled, but no matter what she tried, Rocky wouldn't lift his leg. The problem wasn't her technique, it was her intention. Her body language made it clear: she didn't really want the leg. She wasn't asking like she meant it.

After confirming that fear wasn't holding her back, I gently encouraged her to ask with real purpose, to act as if she truly wanted to be holding that leg, and to stay with it until he responded. On the sixth try, something shifted. Olivia walked up, clear and confident, and asked Rocky for his leg. This time, he lifted it easily.

Another client, Christopher, had a different kind of experience. He successfully asked Rocky for one leg, then, on his own, decided to test himself by switching sides and asking for the other. No one had done that before, but I let him follow his curiosity. Sure enough, on the other side, Rocky refused to lift his leg.

We worked through it together, with my usual reminder to "Ask Like You Mean It." Eventually, he succeeded. In our conversation afterward, Christopher explained that the first leg had come so easily that he doubted whether it was truly a response to his ask, or just

Rocky going through the motions. He needed to be sure Rocky was responding to him, not simply doing what he thought was expected.

That uncertainty, however subtle, showed up in his body language, and Rocky felt it. Once he clarified his intention, and his energy matched his ask, Rocky gave him the leg without hesitation.

These moments are powerful reminders that horses read us clearly. They don't respond to what we say or do alone, they respond to what we mean. And when we bring clarity, presence, and genuine intention into the ask, when we prove to them that we are good leaders, they almost always say yes.

In the story about my sister and the BBQ, my first invitation was not solid; I did not ask like I meant it. When we talked it through and I understood how it felt to her, I was able to deliver a much more invested invitation.

Can I Say No?

Together with "Asking Like You Mean It," working with horses helps remind me that saying no is a necessary part of being clear and setting boundaries. I have no problem saying no to a horse, but sometimes struggle to say no to family and friends.

One day a friend invited me to a function she was hosting at her house. I don't remember the exact details, but I do remember clearly that I did not want to go. Not because I had something else scheduled or a legitimate conflict, I just didn't feel like it.

Instead of being honest, I started piling on excuses: "I'm too busy." "I have work to do." "I'm helping my child with something." All of those could have been true in a general sense, but they weren't the real reason. The truth was simple: I just didn't want to go.

In this case, my friend really wanted me there. She asked with intention. Unfortunately, she didn't allow me to politely decline. She kept offering solutions, trying to remove the obstacles I was putting up. She even offered to change the time of her party to accommodate me.

At that point, I finally had to say, "Please, I'm trying to say no thank you, and I need you to accept that." She eventually did, but it was an awkward and uncomfortable exchange. She felt hurt, and I felt guilty.

Horses aren't nearly this complicated. They prefer a simple, honest yes or no. They don't need an explanation, a justification, or a backstory. I'm trying to learn from that.

Why do we feel the need to explain ourselves when we say no? I often catch myself before launching into a lengthy explanation about why I can or can't do something. The truth is, just because someone invites me doesn't mean I have to go. "No, thank you," is a complete sentence. Most of us need more practice saying no, and we need more practice hearing no without getting offended.

This comes up all the time in my work with horses, especially when we're asking for something vulnerable, like a leg. Asking a horse to lift its leg isn't just a physical request, it's a question that requires trust, clarity, and mutual respect. Just like in human relationships, sometimes the answer is no.

When a horse says no, it doesn't come with a long explanation. There's no backstory, no apology, no awkwardness. The horse simply doesn't lift the leg. Maybe it shifts its weight, walks away, or continues to stand still. The horse's response is direct, and it's honest. Horses are remarkably clear about their boundaries.

What's fascinating is how people respond to that no. Some keep asking more forcefully. Others retreat, uncertain or embarrassed. Very few pause to consider why the horse said no, and even fewer know how to honor that no while staying in the conversation. Sometimes the horse isn't ready. Sometimes we weren't clear. Sometimes we didn't ask like we meant it. Learning to accept a no without reacting is a skill. So is knowing when and how to try again with better timing, intention, and respect.

I see it mirrored in daily life, too. We're conditioned to smooth things over, to say yes when we mean no, and to make up stories so our boundaries are more acceptable. We hesitate to say, "I don't want to," because we're afraid it will hurt someone or seem rude. But isn't it more respectful to be honest, just as a horse is?

I once had a client who kept asking one of my horses for its leg, over and over. The horse wasn't agitated, just unwilling. The client grew flustered and said, "Why won't he let me?"

I don't always know exactly why a horse is responding a certain way, but I can help the client work out a different approach. I asked the client to stand up, take a deep breath and let it out. Then I encouraged the client to relax, then to ask again. I suggested that she stand for a second next to the horse, run her hand down his leg, and then proceed.

That moment shifted everything. She took a step back, took a breath, and tried again with a new tone, clear, respectful, and with a willingness to accept any answer. The horse gave her his leg.

That's what horses teach us if we're willing to listen: how to ask clearly, how to honor a no, and how to stay present enough to try again without force or fear. Saying no is part of a healthy relationship, human or horse. So is hearing it.

In a world that often pushes us to always say yes, I'm finding that practicing clear, compassionate boundaries in the round pen is one of the most powerful lessons of all. It is obvious that for safety, we have to set clear boundaries with horses. They are, after all, large animals that could hurt us physically. Setting emotional boundaries is harder, but even more necessary, some might argue.

Was That a Question?

Julia is a lady who was part-leasing Rocky. She had had some horse experience as a younger girl, so she was not a complete novice. She was comfortable bringing Rocky in from the field, grooming him and taking him for walks and grazing, and generally spending time with him. One day she approached me and said, "Something strange is going on. I cannot get Rocky out of his field anymore." She would show up at the barn, get his halter and lead rope, go out into the field and put it on him but then he would walk halfway to the barn and stop dead in his tracks. She pulled and pulled, but he would not budge. I could not understand what was going on, so I asked her to demonstrate for me.

She went out to the field, put Rocky's halter on and started walking back to the barn with him. Every few steps she would turn around and look at Rocky, as though making sure he was still at the end of the rope. After a few times of doing that, Rocky simply stopped. It was such an interesting interaction, but I could see right away what was going on. I had this explanation for Julia:

"Every time you turn around and look at him, it is as if you are asking him if he wants to continue. You have turned the directive into a question, and ultimately his answer is no, so he stops and plants his feet." I asked her to start walking, with a little tension on the lead rope, and to *not turn around*. I asked her to walk all the way to the gate. She did, and so did Rocky, with no hesitation.

She asked like she meant it. The intention should be: "I put this halter on you, and I lead you out of the pasture. I expect you to follow me. It is not a question that needs your answer. It is an instruction that expects your compliance." None of that needs to be emotional or combative, only direct and clear.

There are so many leadership and parenting correlations here. There are certainly times when situations can be collaborative, but there are also times when clear, intentional direction is needed. The rule of "Ask Like You Mean It" applies not just in asking for Rocky's leg, but in asking him to follow.

After her success with Rocky, I challenged Julia to think about times in her life, whether at home or at work, where her ask might not be clear, intentional, and confident. The lesson here was not about Rocky at all; it was about Julia. Could she use this lesson to help her communicate in a more effective manner? Could this help improve any relationships in her life?

Tug of War

I've seen people get into what I can only call a tug-of-war with horses. Maybe it starts with asking for a leg, or trying to lead the horse somewhere it doesn't want to go. They pull, the horse resists, and suddenly it becomes a contest of strength. But in a physical match between a human and a 1,000-pound animal, we already know who's going to win, and it won't be the human.

That's why I avoid these situations entirely. One of the core principles of good horsemanship is learning to achieve results with as little physical effort as possible. Horses are incredibly reasonable animals. They aren't looking for a fight. If we approach them with clarity, intention, and fairness, they're usually willing to meet us halfway, or more. It's not about overpowering them; it's about communicating in a way that makes sense to them. As prey animals living in our world, they look to us for good leadership, but they'll definitely let us know when we fall short.

This dynamic shows up in human relationships, too. We've all seen a tug-of-war between toddlers and parents, teenagers and authority figures, bosses and employees, even between adult children and their parents. The more one side pulls, the more the other resists. It becomes about winning, not understanding. No one truly wins in that kind of standoff.

So, what does asking a horse for his leg teach us? It teaches us that when we demand instead of ask, when we push instead of listen, we create resistance and avoidance. Avoidance is not good leadership. If a horse says no, yanking on the leg will only make things worse. But if we pause, reassess, and come back with clearer intention and a willingness to listen, we often find the horse is more willing to say yes.

That lesson carries directly into parenting and leadership. When we engage in power struggles, we often stop listening. We focus on compliance instead of connection. When we set clear boundaries with kindness, and ask rather than demand, we open the door to cooperation, rather than conflict.

It's not weakness to step back and re-frame the conversation. As with the story of my daughter's tattoo, I learned that listening and finding a win/win for both sides helped leave the lines of communication open. In fact, it takes strength and consideration to resist getting into a tug-of-war and instead create space for mutual understanding. Horses show us this all the time. They don't engage in a battle they know isn't necessary.

Many years ago, while I was working full-time in Washington D.C., I often noticed ongoing friction between the engineering and accounting departments in the company I was working for. Most of the friction stemmed from issues around contract compliance and budgeting. The engineers were focused on doing the technical work, but they weren't always great at tracking spending or submitting deliverables on time.

At that point in my life, I was ready for a change. I had two young children at home and was looking for a better balance between work and family. I was working in the marketing department, handling the financial components of contract bids, which often meant late nights and weekend hours.

When I saw the growing tension between engineering and accounting, I also saw an opportunity. I pitched a new role to the COO: a liaison who could bridge the gap between the two departments. Someone who would oversee budgeting, contract compliance, and scheduling. It was also a position that could be accomplished on a part-time basis.

He agreed, and the company created a Project Administrator position for me.

I loved that job. It combined my organizational strengths with my ability to navigate interpersonal dynamics. I didn't mind absorbing a bit of the frustration from both sides if it meant easing the tension overall. The tug-of-war ended, not because one side won, but because we changed the way we worked together.

That situation taught me the same lesson horses have taught me for years: when you find yourself in a tug-of-war, the smartest move may be to let go of the rope. Stop fighting. That is not the same as giving up, it's releasing the pressure and tension long enough to invite cooperation and to try to find the win/win for both sides.

Ask, Don't Bribe

Horses are highly food motivated. Carrots, apples, and other treats can be helpful tools for training. There is a distinction between using a treat as a *reward* and using it as a *bribe*. That distinction defines whether we are communicating clearly or manipulating their behavior. When a treat is used as a bribe, the communication breaks down. It stops being about relationship and starts being about transaction, a fine line that has deeper implications.

A treat offered after a job well done is a "thank you." A treat waved in the air to get compliance is a negotiation. That may sound like a small distinction, but it matters, a lot. Bribes come *before* an action to elicit a response; rewards *follow* the response and good behavior.

When I walk into the field to call a horse, I may have a carrot in my pocket, but I do not show it. I do not use it to lure him in. I want the connection to come first. The carrot is optional. Similarly, I want my horse to load onto the trailer because I've asked him to, because he trusts me and understands the request, not because I'm shaking a bucket of grain at the top of the ramp, hoping to lure him in. There is nothing wrong with offering a treat as a thank you, a gesture of appreciation after a job well done. When treats become the main tool for persuasion, then we are no longer building a relationship of mutual respect, we're bribing.

This is something I stress with all my clients. Treats should come *after* the connection, not *instead* of it.

Samantha was a lovely client who carried a bag of carrots to every session. She loved working with Rocky, one of my sweetest and gentlest horses. Samantha was convinced that he would only come to her if she had a treat visible in her hand. If she walked out empty-handed, she believed Rocky would ignore her.

With Samantha, I could see we needed to work on her self-limiting beliefs and how they affected her relationships. I gently encouraged her to try something different: to leave the carrots in her pocket. To step into the field with presence, with confidence, with the idea that she, herself, was enough. It was hard getting her to believe it.

The true work wasn't about getting Rocky to come, or to give up his leg, it was about Samantha believing that she was worth approaching, spending time with, and listening to. That brought up a flood of insecurity in her, and a question many of us carry through life:

Am I enough?

Enough to draw my horse to me, just as I am, without tricks or bribes?

Enough to draw my children to me, without incentives, negotiations or rewards?

Enough to lead, to guide, to invite connection from a place of vulnerability and authenticity?

I used to offer my children money for good grades: ten dollars for every A. At the time, I didn't know what else to do. I wanted to motivate them. I wanted them to care. Still, it bothered me. I knew in my gut that I wasn't instilling self-motivation, I was just buying results. Like so many parents, I was unsure how to motivate them without dangling a carrot.

The deeper hope, of course, was that they would want to do well for their own reasons. That they would feel a sense of personal responsibility and pride. That they would connect their effort with the life they wanted to build.

I tried a few different approaches, but they all felt manipulative. I finally gave up and told my children my frustrations. I explained that I didn't want to "buy" their grades, that I wanted them to want to do better for their own sake. It felt good to be open and transparent, and they confessed that the money was not actually a motivator; the kids who did well just got money on top of good grades, and the kids who struggled resented that good grades and rewards came easier for their siblings. The bribing was actually having a negative impact.

Real leadership, with horses, children or colleagues, isn't about control. It's not about manipulating behavior with rewards or punishments. It's about connection. Consistency. Presence. Trust.

We don't have to bribe the ones we love. We can ask, invite, lead, and support. We can work on deepening individual relationships. We can remember to ask, not bribe.

What does this look like at work? In the workplace, the same distinction shows up between genuine leadership and short-term management responses. If every interaction requires a reward, there is no real leadership going on. It is important, however, to recognize that both incentives (bribes) and rewards are motivators; but when and how often they are used is key.

If you set up the expectation that every assignment will lead to a reward, the culture turns transactional. Employees who are bribed to do their jobs may start to do the bare minimum for the payout instead of feeling connected to the bigger mission. The leader's real goals of building trust, inspiring vision, and creating a sense of belonging can be undermined by using bribery.

Contrast that with leaders who communicate clearly, set expectations, and celebrate effort after the fact. A sincere "thank you," recognition in front of peers, or an opportunity to grow professionally can go further than money on the table (a big assumption here is that employees are being fairly compensated in the first place).

Just like with horses, the reward should follow the action, not precede it. Connection before transaction.

EXERCISE 4: The Magnet

I remember as a child playing with magnets, holding the like poles together, then holding the unlike poles together, and feeling that strange push and pull. There was a clear energy in the air between them: repulsion, then attraction.

Working with horses can feel just like that. You learn to sense the invisible connection between you and the horse, the same magnetic push and pull. All the coaching work at my farm is done without ropes and mostly without any physical contact. We're working at liberty, relying solely on the energy around us. We learn to feel

The Magnet is the culmination of the first three exercises, and a powerful test of connection. Here we reflect on the values we lead with and the kind of energy we radiate. Are we someone others want to follow...or someone they feel obligated to?

each other's presence, and the difference between drawing in and repelling.

Can a 1,000-pound horse follow a person around like a big puppy? The Magnet exercise lets us know if we accomplished our goals with the first three exercises. There's a reason this exercise comes last. We have to go through the first three exercises to build a relationship with the horse and earn his trust. We need to find a common language. You wouldn't step into a round pen for the first time and expect a horse to follow you around instantaneously. Like any meaningful relationship, it takes time and connection. You set up the building blocks of those initial exercises, until a foundation of trust and communication is in place.

After we've established leadership, communication, and trust through the first three exercises, this final test asks: Will the horse willingly cede authority and follow the human around the round pen? In the Western world of horsemanship, this is often called the "join-up." It means just what it sounds like: will the horse join with the human, approaching, connecting, and waiting calmly for direction.

Once that connection is made, I ask participants to simply walk forward and feel whether the horse is following. The instinct is often to turn around and look. Trusting that energetic connection is unfamiliar to most people, and they doubt it's possible. Yet nine times out of ten, the horse is following. Helping humans learn to trust that feeling is one of the loveliest parts of the work.

Ultimately, the goal is to learn how to establish this kind of connection with other people, whether at work or at home.

ROUND PEN SESSIONS • SECTION III

That's Not How Humans Walk

During one session, everything was going beautifully. Lisa, the client, had successfully worked her way through the first three exercises and had gotten Rocky to join up with her in the center of the round pen. I prompted her to walk around the pen and see if he would stay connected, if she could feel his presence without turning around to check.

She started walking, and sure enough, Rocky followed. But then she began moving very tentatively, very slowly. She put one foot down, then picked her other foot up, carefully placing each foot in front of the other, almost in slow motion. I gently encouraged her a few times: "Walk at a normal pace. Stand up straight. Walk like you're out on a hike." But she continued her strange, robotic, slow-motion walk. Eventually, Rocky stopped following. The connection was lost.

Lisa turned to me for guidance.

"Why are you walking like that?" I asked.

"I just want to make sure he can follow me," she said.

"Horses know how humans walk," I replied. "And that's not it."

Rocky was confused by her overly cautious walk and decided to disengage. No connection, no follow.

After a good laugh, Lisa tried again, this time walking with a more natural gait. Rocky happily followed, and we were able to focus on the feeling of his presence behind her. He needed to stop when she stopped, go forward when she went forward, and turn when she turned, all at a normal human-like pace.

For Lisa, learning to trust Rocky's presence around her turned out to be the most enlightening part of the day. Her instinct was still to turn and check, a sign she hadn't fully trusted her own leadership, or his acceptance of it. Once she did, the connection deepened.

During another session, the client, Bill, was very abrupt with his instructions to Ace. After a few minutes of what felt like a very choppy and abrasive interaction, Ace completely shut down and refused to follow. Bill was frustrated and didn't know how to proceed. I often try to let clients figure things out for themselves before intervening, but I could see that both horse and human were stuck.

Bill's frustration resulted in his giving off negative energy; Ace felt it and did not want to follow him. Seems obvious right? Who wants to follow someone who that is abrupt and negative? The beauty of working with horses in this way is that they can choose to not follow; they are not bound by a boss/employee or parent/child relationship. This immediate feedback gives us a clue as to how others feel about our leadership/parenting skills, and we can thereby make some useful adjustments.

Bill's session and difficulty with The Magnet exercise reminded me of a constant battle that I had had with my supervisors, in one of my corporate jobs. My department was in charge of putting together contract bids for private sector as well as government jobs. At times, it felt like we would bid on any RFP (Request for Proposal) that came through the door. It was exhausting. Many times, the decision to bid on a contract was made at the last minute, which meant working late into the night and on weekends. There was no focus. Finally, the department heads got together, and new, clearer policies were put in place. We became more selective about what to bid on, and the yes/no decision was made earlier in the process. Some of the information that went into the proposals was made standard (company history, strengths, compliance paperwork, etc.) so that we did not have to re-invent the process every time.

With Bill and Ace, Bill needed to take the time to walk forward normally so that Ace could get used to following him. There was no need for Bill to make abrupt changes in his direction and/or speed. In sports, quick reactivity is good, but in everyday life situations, most people need more guidance, more notice of what's coming. Without that preparation, employees can feel disrespected and taken advantage of. Predictability often provides stability.

At home, some children react well to quick changes in plans, others do not. With five children, I had a little of both. Some of my kids didn't mind last-minute changes; others needed to know at the beginning of the day what the plan was for the whole day. Knowing these differences in personalities can help establish better communication and create more peaceful interactions. Understanding what individuals need will pave the way for more peaceful interactions.

Block, Don't Punch

One day, I was working with a client named Janet who loved The Magnet exercise, but she hadn't yet grasped all the subtleties involved. We had worked our way through the first three exercises, and Janet was feeling confident. But, for Magnet, once she had Rocky connected and following her, she struggled to maintain her physical boundaries. Rocky kept walking beside her, slowly leaning in and nudging her toward the fence, until eventually she was climbing up onto it just to get space.

I asked Janet to walk next to Rocky again, but this time to maintain her personal bubble. I told her to lift her arms, bent at the elbows, and turn in a full circle. That is the space she needed to protect, her bubble, even when Rocky was right beside or behind her.

They set off again, but just like before, Rocky drifted closer and began pressing her toward the fence.

"Arms up!" I called out.

Janet lifted her arms, but instead of creating a boundary, she started petting Rocky!

"That's going to make him think it's okay," I pointed out. "You're reinforcing the wrong behavior. It's the opposite of what we want."

Janet started over. "Put your arms up and protect your bubble," I said again.

"I just don't want to be mean," she replied. "It feels like you are asking me to punch him."

It became clear that, in life, Janet had difficulty setting boundaries. Saying no or disagreeing with others made her deeply uncomfortable.

What an incredible opportunity this was for her to explore the difference in energy between setting boundaries and letting things build up until they became emotional or argumentative.

Setting boundaries isn't about aggression; it's about clarity. It's like putting up a block, not throwing a punch. The energy is grounded, calm, and intentional. It's simply about making clear what's acceptable and what's not. When done early and clearly, it helps avoid confusion and prevents future conflict.

Setting a boundary with a horse simply helps him understand what is expected. As we've learned, horses, being highly perceptive herd animals, are very much in tune with the energy and intention of those around them. When we are clear and consistent in our cues, most horses are relieved to know where the lines are, because clarity reduces anxiety and fosters trust. Without boundaries, they're left guessing, which can lead to pushiness, shutdown, or erratic behavior. Boundaries aren't about punishment or control; they're about communication and mutual respect.

The same is true for children. When kids know their boundaries, it's easier for them to operate within them, and easier for caregivers to notice and respond when they don't. Clear limits create emotional safety. Children thrive when adults hold firm, loving limits that are predictable and fair. Adele Faber and Elaine Mazlish, in their book, *How to Talk So Kids Will Listen & Listen So Kids Will Talk*, emphasize the importance of setting boundaries with empathy and clarity, acknowledging a child's feelings while still holding firmly to limits. I found this book as well as their book *Siblings Without Rivalry*, immensely helpful while I was raising my children. I was often overwrought and not sure what was the best way to parent. Reaching out for help and guidance helped me understand and re-think many of the traditional parenting models. Working with the horses added to that unconventional approach; as a spectator in one of my clinics, my youngest daughter laughingly said, "Oh, Mom, I see you raised me like you trained the horse!"

Like parenting, in the leadership realm, individuals and teams function best when expectations, roles, and goals are clearly defined. Without structure, people may feel uncertain or even fearful, leading to decreased productivity and increased tension. In her book, *Dare to Lead*, Brené Brown emphasizes that "clear is kind," meaning that the most compassionate and effective leaders are those who offer clarity around expectations, responsibilities, and accountability. Boundaries in the workplace aren't rigid rules; they're agreements that foster trust, autonomy, and performance. When boundaries are inconsistent or unclear, employees may feel confused, undervalued, or frustrated, which undermines engagement and morale.

We are often unaware when we don't have clear boundaries, so working with horses can be very helpful in this context because their feedback is immediate. When a horse is confused or unsure, he'll often stop and disengage in response. At that point, we need to figure out what we are doing (or not doing) to elicit that response. Another benefit is that the interaction will not proceed until we get it right; the horse will not just "go-along." With people, we sometimes continue down the wrong path for too long.

When I say, "Block, don't punch," I often invite clients to reflect on a past argument. I ask, "Was there a point in that conversation where you could have blocked or redirected the energy, before it escalated into a full-blown argument?" Often, they can identify such a point. Setting boundaries, speaking your mind calmly, or simply asking a thoughtful question can disrupt the downward spiral into conflict. These small interventions help shift the momentum before things get too heated. It's not always easy, and it takes practice, but with awareness and intention, we can learn to engage without fueling the fire.

As Janet worked through this exercise with Rocky, we had a powerful conversation about setting both emotional and physical boundaries. With practice, she was able to raise her arms and gently block Rocky's nudges, without feeling she was being mean or aggressive. She began to understand that holding her ground wasn't about confrontation; it was about communication.

Did Rocky know Janet needed to learn that lesson or was he just testing his boundaries?

Why Trick Him?

Clients are often surprised to find themselves leading a horse without ropes, halters, or leashes, just walking together freely. The men, in particular, seem to love this exercise. I've asked many of them why, and the most common answer is some version of "I can't believe a 1,000-pound animal is following me around like a big puppy."

It was a beautiful, sunny spring day when John and Mary, a husband and wife, visited the farm for a session. They were both engaged in the exercises, learning about themselves, and picking up insights about how they communicated. Ace, was in great form; attentive and, at times, even affectionate. He's not usually my most demonstrative horse, so it was lovely to see him reaching out for connection.

Mary went first. She took direction well, moved through all four exercises, and made meaningful connections between what she was learning with Ace, and in her own life. Then it was John's turn. He did well with the first three exercises, he noticed where he wasn't being clear or direct, made adjustments, and saw success.

Then came the final exercise: The Magnet.

For some reason, John decided he wanted to "test" the connection. Instead of walking in a straight, intentional line, he began zigzagging all over the round pen. At first, Ace followed. But eventually, he stopped. John's energy rose, clearly frustrated, but Ace still wouldn't move. Ace stomped his foot, then slowly turned and walked away.

"Why did he stop following me?" John asked, genuinely confused.

"Well," I said, "why were you zig-zagging so much? Wasn't he already following you?"

"I wanted to test him," John replied.

The only explanation I could offer was that Ace felt tricked, or maybe just confused. From Ace's perspective, the sudden changes in direction had no clear purpose. The connection stopped making sense, so he opted out.

In that moment, all the progress John had made in the earlier exercises faded. It became clear that while he had been doing the work, he hadn't fully absorbed the underlying principles.

Connection needs to be authentic, clear, and reasonable. Good leadership doesn't feel erratic or reactive. It's intentional. It flows. Horses—and people—respond best when they trust where you're going.

Another point John mentioned is that he didn't know what was next. He was just "winging it." Ace didn't like that. Who does? It is very hard for people to follow you if they don't trust your leadership; if they don't trust that you know what you are doing. When John zig-zagged around the pen, Ace must have thought that John didn't know what he was doing.

Don't Worry, He's Following

During The Magnet exercise, I often see clients stop and turn around mid-walk to make sure the horse is still behind them.

"He's still there, I promise. Keep walking!" I gently call out.

I don't want the client to break the connection, until *they decide to*. By this point in the session, the connection isn't only physical, it's also mental. The client needs to trust that the horse is following based on everything they've built together. That kind of trust can be hard to believe in.

And, just as important to forming a connection, is being able to release one. Up until this point, all the focus has been on how to get the horse to connect with us through communication and how all those lessons in communication translate into an individual's life, with the goal of improving relationships.

How do we release connections? We get stuck in our own stories, stories that say, "This won't work," "They don't care," or "I'm not good enough." We create mental loops and continuously repeat them. If a client is convinced the horse isn't following, they'll keep turning around…and eventually, the horse won't follow. They've broken the moment, the forward momentum, not because the horse changed, but because the client couldn't let go of their disbelief.

Getting stuck isn't always about facts. It's about what we believe to be true.

If you're familiar with the work of Byron Katie, you know she offers a powerful process for getting unstuck from these mental loops. My personal understanding of her method, "The Work," invites us to take a thought we're holding tightly, maybe even painfully, and turn it around. Literally. Flip it. Try on the opposite thought. Sit with it. Let it loosen the grip of the original belief. Think of it like a pendulum swinging to the other side, with the hope that it will settle somewhere in the middle. It works!

I experienced this firsthand. After a breakup, I found myself caught in a cycle of anger and resentment. My ex had started dating again almost immediately, and I told myself, "He must not have cared about me at all." That thought gnawed at me. It fueled the narrative that our relationship had meant nothing to him and kept me stuck in pain and anger.

Around this time, I attended a workshop where we were asked to write down a statement we were holding onto, and then write down the opposite. My statement that I was stuck to was that he should not have started dating again. Following the instructions to write the opposite of my stuck statement, I wrote:

Of course he should be dating.
He should date 1,000 women.
He should have a new date every night.
He should fall in love with someone else.

I'll admit, it felt ridiculous, and infuriating, at first. Some of those lines were followed by a few choice words. Then I had to admit that something was shifting. I started to release my resentment. That practice didn't instantly erase my hurt, but it gave me another path. When the old thoughts resurfaced, I had a way to challenge them, and let them go.

When we stay stuck in one story, we limit what's possible. Whether it's a horse not following, a partner moving on, or a colleague's reaction at work, we often respond based on what we believe, not what's actually happening.

So, the next time you find yourself circling in a loop, ask:

"Is this true? Or is this just the story I'm stuck in?" And if you can, try thinking the opposite.

In the round pen, during The Magnet, the client often doesn't realize that their belief that the horse is actually following is key. When they don't believe it, they get stuck, and the momentum is broken. Thankfully, talking through the hesitations usually settles the disbelief, and with guidance the horse is ready to reconnect and follow.

Section III: Reflection Prompts

- Can you find the balance between talking and listening?
- Do you "Ask Like You Mean It"?
- Are you someone others are drawn to, or someone they avoid?

SECTION IV

Stories from Clients

When I started the Horse and People Project, I wasn't sure other people would *get it*. I knew that being around the horses was having a profound effect on me and my relationships, but would these same lessons help others? The short answer is yes!

Every session tells its own story. Sometimes it's a quiet shift, sometimes a big "aha" moment, and sometimes the client walks away with more profound insights that they keep to themselves.

Every time someone steps into the round pen, I get to be part of someone else's experience. I am constantly reminded that the work is much more about the people than about the horses. The conversations, the epiphanies, and yes, sometimes the tears, are what make each session unique. A few of my clients have generously offered to put their experiences into words, and I'm so grateful to share them here. These stories are not just about what happened in the pen; they're about finding clarity, building trust, and discovering something new about ourselves.

Sue Balentine

Rocky was my friend. He was a beautiful boy, ginger and cream, with a textured coat that changed with the seasons. He was a pleasure to groom because he enjoyed it, and because the reveal was so satisfying. He had one blue eye and one brown; somehow, that gave him a mystical aspect. I didn't ride him; despite his tolerance of me, it was too steep a learning curve. We settled into a rhythm of greeting, letting him out to graze, grooming, and simply hanging out together. He would often head up to the greener hay field above the fencing to graze, checking by looking back, to see if I was following. I know he enjoyed the freedom, and he seemed to enjoy the company. It was what we did together. I loved watching him, and I learned the language of "horse" by seeing how he related to the other horses, and they, to him. He was the one to yield to the others.

Rocky was calm. Being around him could change my inner experience: I became calmer, too. I could feel his steadiness and his acceptance, which was a great gift.

In the beginning of our time together, I didn't know what I was doing, and he knew that! He ignored me when I asked him to come with me. Over time, he learned he could trust me, and he knew what we did together was enjoyable, so he was very tuned in, and would come to me without being asked. At the end of our time together in the fields, I always gave him some carrots—cooked carrots, for the last year or so, because his teeth were so worn. He gobbled them up! Rocky loved to eat.

My world became bigger during the three-plus years we hung out at the barn, yet it was a time of such peaceful respite. I cherished our time together and feel honored to have met such a wise creature. He was a teacher of energy and how it flows between beings. I knew about energy because of my Reiki training and many experiences and travels I've had that focused upon energy. And, still, Rocky showed me the capacity of the horse to absorb emotion and soothe others just by being fully present. I can feel him with me now, even though he no longer resides in his beautiful body.

What a wonder this life is! Thank you, Rocky, for sharing yours.

Tedy Kamenova

When I signed up for my initial session with Maria and the Horse and People Project, I wasn't sure what to expect. I was a little nervous. "What if the horse doesn't like me? What if it doesn't follow my directions? What would this mean about the person I am?" All those thoughts flooded my mind as I was on my way to the session.

Upon arrival, Maria greeted us and walked us through everything we were about to experience. She explained how to communicate effectively with the horse and give clear directions, also how to read the different responses and relate them to different scenarios in our life. The only thing we did not know was how the horse would react.

Once I started working with the horse, Maria was there to guide me through every step, and I was surprised to see that the horse was working with me and following my directions. Before the session, I did not believe in myself and was pretty sure the horse was not going to cooperate. "I needed a horse to show me that I can believe in myself, and I can lead! That I can communicate effectively!" I thought.

At some point, Maria told me to press the horse in the chest with my fingers so the horse would take a few steps back. "Would it hurt?" I asked, and Maria assured me that it would not hurt the horse.

When I pressed the horse's chest, he did not budge. I was being "too gentle" and trying not to hurt him, and I was not communicating clearly. Maria asked me to press like I mean it, and to my surprise when I did, the horse took a few steps back.

Wow, that was it! I realized that has been my problem when communicating with others, professionally and personally. I have been trying not to hurt their feelings and therefore, not communicating clearly.

That was such a pivotal moment in my life! From then on, when someone asks me to do something that I do not want to do, whether a co-worker, manager, family member or friend, I simply and clearly say, "No." That has lifted a huge weight off of me and has left me with more time and energy for the things I love doing.

Denise Golden

I visited the Horse and People Project hoping to gain insight that could support me in my role as a supervisor and trainer. I was both excited and nervous when stepping into the ring with the horse; I wanted to do everything just right from the start. But what unfolded that day, and in the days that followed, was so much more than I ever expected.

My husband and I attended the event together, each for different reasons, both career focused. But I left with a deeper understanding of how to communicate—not just professionally, but with my husband

and our children, as well. That first visit was through a networking group exploring ways we could support one another, and for me, it was also a special treat since I've always loved horses.

As Maria shared stories about supervisors and supervisees, I could clearly picture colleagues and how this experience could benefit them. Then she spoke about her son and a moment they shared: how he hesitated to enter the room while she was enjoying her coffee. That story struck me deeply. I thought about how I greet my own son after school, often jumping right into questions about his day without recognizing his need to decompress. I realized I'd been missing important signals.

That same afternoon, I apologized to my son when I picked him up. I used one of the techniques Maria described: asking if I could continue playing my podcast so he could relax, giving him space to talk when he was ready. I've done this ever since, and our connection has grown stronger.

It also made me reflect on how I communicate with my husband. I often dominate the conversation, downloading my day and announcing our plans, leaving little room for his processing. I realized I needed to change. Despite all my professional training in communication and emotional intelligence, I hadn't been practicing those tools at home. I felt like a hypocrite, teaching others how to get it right while missing the mark in my personal space.

On our third visit, we brought our son to an open house. As Maria spoke, he leaned over and whispered, "Mom, I hope Dad is listening. He could learn a lot about our relationship." My son was just fifteen, but his words were wise. Every time I attend events at the Horse and People Project, I walk away with more tools that I'm putting into practice.

Our marriage has strengthened. We now respect our individual processing styles and value our time together in a more mindful way. I've learned, through the horses, that energy and trust are at the heart of every relationship. My husband needs time to sit with things before speaking, and I'm learning to give him that space. Like the horse, he responds best when the signals are clear, calm, and consistent.

I know I'm a work in progress, but thanks to the Horse and People Project, I continue to grow as a person, a partner, and a parent. I'm deeply grateful to Maria and the transformative experience she's created.

Thank you, Maria!

Klara Tselenchuk

What prompted you to visit the Horse & People Project?

I was really curious about the idea of learning and healing through horses. I had also had some past experiences with horses that left me feeling nervous, so a part of me wanted to face that and see if something could shift. I've done a lot of work around connecting with nature, and this felt like the perfect next step.

What were your initial feelings about the visit? What kind of day was it? Was it a special occasion?

I felt both excited and a little anxious! It wasn't tied to any special event, but I had gathered a group of people to do this together as part of my work around helping people connect to themselves and nature. I wasn't totally sure what to expect, but I went in with an open heart, and honestly, it turned into such a beautiful and meaningful day.

Did you go with other people?

Yep! I went with a small group, and it felt so supportive to be there together. Everyone came with their own energy and stories, but somehow the experience with the horses brought us all into the same kind of learning space. There was something really powerful about doing it as a group.

Which horse did you work/play with?

I worked with Rocky.

Were any of the exercises more pertinent to you specifically?

Definitely the one where we acted like a magnet. The idea was to invite Rocky to follow us, without pulling or pushing. It made me think about how I show up with my kids and in my work. I realized how often I try to control or explain too much, when really, leadership and trust come from being calm and clear. That exercise will stay with me for a long time.

What emotions did you have while working with the horse?

So many! At first, I was nervous and unsure, but then I felt this sense of wonder and respect. And when Rocky started responding to my energy, I felt this wave of calm confidence. I learned that horses don't fake it, they reflect what's real. And that felt so powerful.

I also loved watching the other people in the group. Observing their interactions was a whole other layer of learning.

Did you learn anything about yourself? Or remember anything about yourself?

Yes, I remembered that I can be clear and grounded. I remembered that I don't have to overthink or second-guess everything. I saw how my own doubt or mixed energy can really shape how I show up, not just with horses, but with my daughters, with clients, with everyone. And that reminder, that energy speaks louder than words, really stuck with me.

Did the emotions/feelings carry throughout the day/week?

Absolutely. I noticed myself pausing more before reacting, especially with my kids. I'd stop and think, "Am I encouraging right now? Or am I nagging?" I felt more grounded in my body, too. It was like something clicked into place.

Were you able to make any changes in your life based on what you learned?

Yes, in little ways that feel really meaningful. I've been more intentional with how I communicate, especially at home. I'm learning to hold space instead of rushing things or trying to control the outcome. And I've been more mindful about not blaming outside circumstances when things go sideways. Instead, I'm asking myself, "What's really going on inside me right now?" This experience reminded me how powerful real connection is.

James M. Golden

While it might seem a bit peculiar to be going to a horse farm and not riding a single horse, it's perhaps even more strange to realize that you've walked away with a changed perspective on how you interact with others. I know I certainly did.

I have been to Maria's farm twice. Once to work with one of her horses through Maria's coaching and prepared lessons, and the other time to listen to Maria speak about her experiences and explain how she uses the horses to teach folks about interpersonal relationships. Months later, I am still taking in some of the lessons I learned and listened to during those visits.

Though I'm still learning to apply some of the lessons in being a father, I often get a reminder that I missed the bar when it comes to something I may say to my son. For example, Maria tells a story about one day catching her son immediately backing out of the room when he noticed that she was in the room. How often do we start our interactions with our children focused on what we feel they need to hear or get done that day, without reminding them first and foremost that we care about them? I know I'm certainly guilty of that. "Hey, it's time to get up now." "Hey, hurry up, it's time to get to school!" and on and on. It's kind of like walking into your office each day and your boss drops a pile of work on your desk without bothering to say hi or anything polite. It won't be long before you resent going to work. From our kids' perspective, it's not really any different. With the horses, Maria eloquently puts this on display. Come at a horse with too many to-dos and too much determination, all hardness and no softness, and the horse will quickly let you know that he's not interested in anything you want him to do.

But there are also lessons for the business world. Ever had a manager who was always micromanaging, never stepping back to let you do your job? Or perhaps you had a manager that was too hands-off, or rather wishy-washy, never clear on what he or she wanted from staff? A horse will quickly let you know when you're being too pushy and demanding, or when he has no idea what you want from him.

Yes, perhaps it sounds cliché, but there truly is a lot we can learn from a horse. If we pay attention, keep an open mind, drop our defenses, and follow Maria's gentle guidance, we can learn about ourselves as parents, as family members, as co-workers, and as managers and leaders. And what could be better than learning all that while outside with a beautiful horse?

If you visit Maria at the Horse and People Project, I guarantee that you will come away with something that you'll carry with you for a long time, if not the rest of your life. I know I have.

Liza Jones

My visit to the Horse and People Project was in celebration of a friend's birthday. A small group of us were there, some having been before, some new to the experience, not knowing entirely what to expect. We went into it with optimism. It was a mild sunny day in February, late morning, when I pulled up to the barn. Our group was circled up at the ring, with Maria and Finn inside. One by one, each person in our group went inside the ring to work with Finn. We each had our own unique experience, despite being given the same instructions by Maria. Exercises included placing our hands on Finn's chest and walking forward a certain number of steps, walking around the ring with Finn at our back shoulder, directing Finn as he galloped around the ring, and lifting up his leg from a standing pose.

When I first stepped into the ring with Finn, I remember the voice in my head saying," So what are we working on?" The voice responded, "Brother". My brother had dated a few women who were horse riders and trainers. I don't have a great relationship with him, so perhaps Finn was trying to help me regulate my nervous system to relate to my brother so that we could communicate better and meet each other on a level playing field.

My experience with Finn was unexpected as he tuned into my nervous system. His reaction was similar to the spiritual alchemist healer I worked with in 2022. What Finn did surprised even Maria; he started yawning continuously. He was releasing stuckness (perhaps hiding as subconscious traumas). His mouth opened wide, he stuck his tongue out, his neck shook from side to side, and up and down. He yawned deeply and loudly like a furiously peaceful release of the body and mind. This went on for a good three to five minutes, at least, and at multiple times throughout the session.

The emotions I had while working with Finn were peaceful, hopeful, calm, inquisitive, loving, and kind. I learned that the living beings on earth, regardless of species (horse or human), connect with unconditional love to raise our collective frequencies and heal our deepest wounds.

It was such a great experience, and now whenever I see a horse or come into contact with one, I think of their big hearts. I remember how Finn helped deepen my capacity by releasing the stuckness and decreasing my anxiety, allowing me to be able to help other humans and living beings honor their truths as a yoga teacher. I'm grateful to have such a unique story to share and be able to connect more deeply with my brother. Thanks, Finn, Maria, the Horse and People Project!

SECTION V

Looking Ahead

When I think back over the many sessions I've had in the round pen, my own journey, and that of my clients, what strikes me the most is not the horses' behavior, but the people's faces when something clicks. There's a moment when the lesson becomes less about the horse and more about the person. Whenever the horse becomes the focus, I remind them, "This is not about the horse, it's about you."

I love being part of a client's aha moment. When they realize, "Oh…this is how I've been showing up with my kids," or, "No wonder my team avoids me." These have always been the moments that matter the most to me: when the horse becomes the mirror, the teacher, the partner in growth. Not only do I keep learning, but I get to witness people step into a new kind of leadership, one rooted not in force, but in clarity, trust, and connection.

I also see a lot of hesitation and skepticism. "What are we going to learn?" and "How is this horse going to help me personally?" are often questions I get. It is a challenge to get people to trust the process, to be open to learning about themselves in an entirely different way. And then there's joy and astonishment after each session, talk, or workshop, when individuals realize how practical and real the lessons are to each of them.

My biggest hope in writing this book is that the reader might see themselves in some of the stories and get a glimpse as to how a situation could be seen through a horse's eyes. One of my editors even commented, "It's full of lessons within lessons!" Throughout the book, there are reflection prompts to inspire personal introspection, and help pinpoint areas where a small change could go a long way in smoothing out an interaction or relationship.

As you close this book, I invite you to carry these lessons forward into your own life. You don't need a round pen or a thousand-pound horse to practice them. You already have daily opportunities: in how you greet your child after a long day, in how you handle a disagreement at work, in how you listen to your partner when they're struggling.

The round pen may be behind you now, but the lessons are only beginning. Horses have shown us that leadership is not about dominance, but about relationship. Not about demanding, but about inviting. Not about power, but about presence.

That is the gift they give us, a way of being that draws others in willingly, like a magnet. My hope is that you'll take this gift with you into the places that matter most: your home, your workplace, your community, and your own heart.

Because in the end, it was never about the horse, it was about you.

Continuing the Journey

Finishing this book isn't the end; I hope it's just the beginning. Just like working with a horse, communication and leadership aren't mastered in a single session; they are built moment by moment, through awareness and practice. Here's a guide to help you keep working with the lessons we explored together.

1. Revisit Lessons from the Core Exercises

THE BACK-UP: Reflect on how you hold yourself; what energy you carry, whether your intention matches your instruction. Where do you need to step forward with clarity and strength? Where can you soften your approach?

THE SEND: Notice when you skip over connecting and dive straight into directing. Do you talk more than you listen? Do you give feedback but are resistant to receiving it?

THE LEG: Ask Like You Mean It! Practice clear, direct communication in your daily life. State your request with intention and allow for the response. Apply this with colleagues, children, or partners, and allow for breathing room before reconnecting.

THE MAGNET: Pay attention to when others follow you willingly. What kind of energy draws people in, and what kind of energy pushes them away?

2. Keep a Reflection Journal

Many people benefit from writing their thoughts down and keeping a journal. Use the reflection prompts above and at the end of the chapters to help find clarity.

3. Practice in Different Arenas

You may not have access to horses and round pens, but think of your life as having its own "round pens":

AT HOME: Try using the lessons learned with your children, partner, friends, or extended family. Notice where clarity or boundaries improve harmony.

AT WORK: Experiment with trust-based leadership and openness to feedback. See how colleagues respond when you invite connection instead of demanding compliance.

WITH YOURSELF: Pay attention to the stories you tell yourself. Can you "flip" a limiting belief and find a new perspective?

4. Return to the Horses

If you ever have the opportunity, step into round pen with a horse! If you are not able to visit the Horse and People Project, try volunteering at a local horse rescue. Horse rescues offer the opportunity for volunteers to connect and learn from many different kinds of horses.

Resources

Brown, Brené. *Dare to Lead: Brave Work. Tough Conversations. Whole Hearts.* New York: Random House, 2018. Explores how vulnerability, empathy, and courageous leadership build stronger teams and more authentic workplaces.

Faber, Adele, and Elaine Mazlish. *Siblings Without Rivalry: How to Help Your Children Live Together So You Can Live Too.* Revised edition. New York: W. W. Norton & Company, 2012. Offers practical tools and empathetic strategies to help parents reduce conflict, foster cooperation, and support healthy, respectful relationships between their children.

Faber, Adele, and Elaine Mazlish. *How to Talk So Kids Will Listen & Listen So Kids Will Talk.* 30th Anniversary Edition. New York: Scribner, 2012. This practical guide offers respectful, compassionate communication strategies that help parents set boundaries, manage conflict, and build stronger, more cooperative relationships with their children.

Fulghum, Robert. *All I Really Need to Know I Learned in Kindergarten: Uncommon Thoughts on Common Things.* New York: Random House, 1988. A reflective collection of essays sharing simple but profound truths about life, drawn from everyday experiences.

Grandin, Temple, and Catherine Johnson. *Animals in Translation: Using the Mysteries of Autism to Decode Animal Behavior.* New York:

Scribner, 2005. A fascinating look at how animals perceive the world, blending neuroscience, animal science, and autism research.

Grandin, Temple, and Catherine Johnson. *Animals Make Us Human: Creating the Best Life for Animals.* New York: Houghton Mifflin Harcourt, 2009. An exploration of animal emotional needs and how to improve the quality of life for animals in our care.

Jones, Janet L. Horse Brain, Human Brain: *The Neuroscience of Horsemanship.* North Pomfret, VT: Trafalgar Square Books, 2020. A neuroscience-based guide to understanding how horses think and how humans can communicate more effectively with them.

Katie, Byron, and Stephen Mitchell. *Loving What Is: Four Questions That Can Change Your Life.* New York: Harmony Books, 2002. Teaches a structured inquiry process to challenge limiting beliefs and shift internal narratives.

Staver, Mike. *Leadership Isn't for Cowards: How to Drive Performance by Challenging People and Confronting Problems.* Hoboken, NJ: John Wiley & Sons, 2012. A practical, tough-love approach to leadership that emphasizes action, accountability, and direct communication.

Tolle, Eckhart. *The Power of Now: A Guide to Spiritual Enlightenment.* Novato, CA: New World Library, 1999. A spiritual guide to mindfulness and present-moment awareness as a path out of mental suffering and ego-driven living.

Pendry, P., & Roeter. "Experimental trial demonstrates positive effects of equine-facilitated learning on child social competence." *Human-Animal Interaction Bulletin.* Vol. 1, No.1. (2013), Pages 1-19. Demonstrated that equine-facilitated learning significantly reduced stress and improved social competence in children through measurable drops in cortisol levels.

PsychCentral. "All About Equine-Assisted Psychotherapy." Last modified June 24, 2022. https://psychcentral.com/health/equine-assisted-psychotherapy Detailed numerous health benefits of being around horses.

HeartMath Institute–Connecting Hearts: Understanding the Research of the Symbiotic Relationship Between Horses and Humans | HeartMath Institute Explored the heart-to-heart electromagnetic synchronization between humans and horses, supporting the idea of emotional and physiological coherence.

Kohanov, Linda. *The Tao of Equus: A Woman's Journey of Healing and Transformation Through the Way of the Horse.* Novato, CA: New World Library, 2001.

Kohanov, Linda. *The Power of the Herd: A Nonpredatory Approach to Social Intelligence, Leadership, and Innovation.* Novato, CA: New World Library, 2013. Introduced the concept of "nonpredatory leadership" using horse behavior to teach presence, congruence, and emotional agility in human leaders.

Acknowledgements

I have always been private about my faith, but there is no denying the impact God has on my life. Every bit of goodness in my life has come from Him, and this book is no exception. One of the greatest gifts He's given me is a love for horses. They've been my steady teachers, my mirrors, and sometimes even my healers. Without them, there wouldn't be lessons to share, stories to tell, or insights to pass on.

To my kids, Gaby, Tommy, Kevin, Lucy and Hannah—thank you for being both my biggest joy and my most important teachers. I know I haven't always gotten it right, but your love and grace keep me learning. I am proud of the people you are becoming, and so grateful to be your mother.

To my writing coach, early supporters, and draft readers, Donna, Sue, Jen, Lu, Gaby, MaryBeth and Luz—thank you for your encouragement and taking the time to read early versions. Your honest feedback helped me see what needed more clarity, and which the stories resonated most.

To my clients and friends, thank you for trusting me with your stories and for allowing me to share some of them here. Your courage and openness have made these lessons real and relatable.

And to you, the reader, thank you for picking up this book. I hope something in these pages meets you right where you are, and maybe helps you see yourself, your work, or your family in a new light.

About the Author

Maria's love of horses began at an early age when she volunteered to work with the U.S. Park Police's mounted unit in New York City.

Throughout childhood, Maria observed horses had a clear ability to convey a message. Though she received her MBA and worked in corporate America for over 20 years, Maria never lost her passion for horses.

Her work is rooted in self-help, self-awareness, personal development, communication, and leadership principles, empowering others to find clarity and growth.

When not at the barn playing with her horses or leading sessions, Maria likes to spend time with her human herd, travel, dance, hike, bike, garden, read and knit. Having lived in a few different states, Maria now calls Maryland her home.

www.ingramcontent.com/pod-product-compliance
Lightning Source LLC
Chambersburg PA
CBHW020502030426
42337CB00011B/205